# WALKLOG

Diary and Guide for the Exercise Walker
First Edition

Don and Debbi Lawrence

*A Division of Howards W. Sams & Company*

Published by Masters Press (a division of Howard W. Sams & Company)
2647 Waterfront Pkwy. E. Drive, Suite 300
Indianapolis, IN 46214

WalkLog: Diary and Guide for the Exercise Walker
First Edition

© 1994 by The Brown Group, Inc., Don Lawrence and Debbi Lawrence
© renewed 1995 by Masters Press

All rights reserved

First Masters Press edition published 1995
10 9 8 7 6 5 4 3 2 1

Printed in the United States of America.

No part of this publication may be reproduced, stored in a retrieval system, or transmitted, in any form or by any means, electronic, mechanical, photocopying, recording, or otherwise, without the prior written permission of Masters Press.

# TABLE OF CONTENTS

About the Authors .................................................................................v
Introduction .......................................................................................vii
NaturalSport, The Walker's Choice .....................................................viii
Walking Statistics ..................................................................................1
Footwear: Key Features for a Walking Shoe .........................................3
Stretching: Warm Up Before You Work Out.........................................5
Stretches...............................................................................................6
Walking Technique: High-Intensity Aerobic Walking............................8
Heart Rate: Let Your Heart Be Your Guide.........................................10
Visualization: What You See is What You Get ....................................13
Nutrition: Enhance Your Exercise from the Inside Out ......................15
Fluids: Walking on Water ...................................................................17
Winter Walking: Weather or Not?......................................................18
Strength: Weight Training & Drills ....................................................19
Injury Prevenion: Injury-Free Walking ...............................................22
Body Sculpturing: Weight Loss Through Fat Loss..............................24
A Sample Walking Program ................................................................26
Commonly Asked Questions on Walking ...........................................28
Your Personal Walking Log.................................................................31
Measurements: How Do You Measure Up?.......................................33
Weekly Mileage at a Glance ................................................................36
Cumulative Mileage Chart ..................................................................38
Pace Chart ..........................................................................................40

**Credits:**
Cover and inside color photographs © 1994 by Brown Group, Inc. except for photo noted as © by Victah Sailer/Agence Shot. Black and white photos © 1994 Sports Log Publishers
Cover design by Suzanne Lincoln
Book design by Catharine Cooper

# Log Your Best

### Give yourself or a friend the best training diaries available!

Masters Press' SportsLog Series is your training accessory partner with its full line of training diaries. Feel free to tell a friend or a training partner about our products and call or write us for more information or to reorder any SportsLog title.

### The SportsLog Series includes:
RunLog           LiftLog
WalkLog          TriLog
CycleLog

### Call (800) 722-2677 to order!
Call toll free in the U.S. or (317) 298-5604 from outside the U.S., or write: Masters Press, 2647 Waterfront Pkwy. E. Drive, Suite 300, Indianapolis, IN 46214. Good luck with your training.

# ABOUT THE AUTHORS

## DEBBI LAWRENCE

Debbi Lawrence was a member of the 1992 Olympic Team in the inaugural women's 10km racewalk, and is a spokeswoman for NaturalSport. In 1991, she won the silver medal at the Pan Am Games and, since then, has broken the American record several times at various racewalking distances. Debbi established the world's fastest indoor time at the metric mile, and to her credit, has won several U.S. National Racewalk Championships. She has represented the U.S. in numerous international competitions. Debbi began her racewalking career in 1981, after successfully competing as a collegiate runner.

## DON LAWRENCE

Don Lawrence is a member of the U.S. National Racewalk Team and was a three-time Olympic Trials finalist in the 20km racewalk. He has represented the U.S. in international racewalking competition, and has been involved with the sport for more than 20 years.

In addition to their racewalking training and competitions, the Lawrences conduct nationwide walking clinics, and consult with NaturalSport footwear on new product development and design.

# INTRODUCTION

One of the greatest aspects of walking for health, fitness or competition is that the benefits are tremendous and the needs are few. Walking is a great way to burn calories and tone muscles, while gaining excellent aerobic condition.

A walking log indicates the "whys" of a successful training period and can provide valuable explanation for illness and injury. It can keep your goals in focus and become a strong motivator and excellent training tool. You will be glad you took the time to chart your progress!

This log book was designed with you, the walker, in mind. Enjoy!

Walk with us,

Don and Debbi Lawrence

# NATURALSPORT®
# THE WALKER'S CHOICE®

NaturalSport is the only brand of women's shoes to focus solely on meeting the needs of walkers. Through the use of state-of-the-art materials and components, NaturalSport offers enhanced comfort technology in a full line of walking shoes for casual, brisk and high-intensity walking.

The design and development of NaturalSport walking shoes is based upon extensive consumer research and laboratory testing. In addition, NaturalSport consults with top racewalkers, such as Don and Debbi Lawrence, to design and wear-test footwear that meets the demands of competitive athletes as well as those of recreational walkers.

Through sponsorships of walking events and of competitive racewalkers, NaturalSport is contributing to the support and growth of the activity of exercise walking, as well as to the sport of racewalking.

NaturalSport advanced the performance of its walking shoes this season with its new NaturalSport Cradle® technology. Cradle technology offers the optimum blend of comfort, support and protection through a unique construction that enhances rebound, cushioning and stability while a woman walks. You can find NaturalSport Cradle technology in a NaturalSport walking shoe that fits your special walking needs: casual walking (C1), brisk exercise walking (C2) and high-intensity aerobic walking (C3).

Representing the ultimate in quality, performance and comfort, NaturalSport is the walker's choice.

NaturalSport is a registered trademark of Brown Group, Inc., St. Louis, MO. The Walker's Choice is a registered trademark of Brown Group, Inc., St. Louis, MO. NaturalSport Cradle is a registered trademark of Brown Group, Inc., St. Louis, MO.

# WALKING STATISTICS

Here are some facts and figures, tips and trivia on the nation's most popular form of exercise:

- In a 1956 racewalking competition, the gold medal 50km racewalker was lost in a corridor of the stadium prior to the competition, and did not find his way to the track until the other walkers were already lined up on the starting line.

- The 6th place finisher in the 1964 Olympic Games 20km walk was Ron Zinn, a U.S. competitor. He died in the Vietnam War less than nine months after attaining this finish at age 26. Today, Ron is honored through the "Outstanding Male and Female Racewalker of the Year" award, which is offered in his name.

- Each foot has 26 bones, 33 joints, 31 tendons, 100 ligaments and thousands of sweat glands. Of the 19 muscles on the foot, 18 are on the bottom.

- A walker's style is as unique as his or her fingerprints and footprints.

- High-heeled shoes cause the Achilles tendon (located vertically from ankle to mid-calf in the back of your leg) to shorten. If you enjoy wearing heels, concentrate on stretching this area, particularly before exercise walking.

- The Olympic racewalking distances are 20 km (12.5 miles) and 50km (31.25 miles) for men, and 10 km (6.25 miles) for women.

- You can increase the value and calorie-burn of your walking exercise by increasing the speed at which you walk (for example, covering a mile in 14 minutes instead of 15) and/or increasing the incline of your path (such as hill walking). Always allow extra rest-days with either hilly or faster walking.

- "Side stitches" sometimes occur when walking too fast, particularly if the muscles of the midsection are not properly stretched or when a hard-to-digest meal has been eaten just before the walk. To relax the stitch, breathe deeply and slow down or stop if necessary.

- A normal person will walk 8,000 - 10,000 steps in a day which translates to approximately 115,000 miles in a lifetime.

- The first sex tests for female athletes occurred in 1968.

- In 1979, the first sanctioned IAAF women's racewalk was held in Eschborn, Spain. The distance was 10km.

- To gain or maintain fitness, exercise at least three times per week. It takes about six weeks for your body to adapt to any new form of exercise. Never increase your walking mileage by more than 10% per week.

- The first Olympic racewalk for women was held in 1992 in Barcelona, Spain at the 25th Summer Olympic Games. The distance: 10 km.

*Tape your favorite motivational photo, or note your goals here.*

# FOOTWEAR: KEY FEATURES FOR A WALKING SHOE

Choose a shoe with comfort, support and protection. A walking shoe is designed with the right amount of cushioning to absorb the shock of the walking step, but also with a certain degree of firmness to rebound the foot back into the stride. Too much cushioning can sap your energy while walking.

A walker should also look for midsole stability to support and protect the foot from unnecessary motion upon hitting the ground. In addition, a flexible forefront comforts the foot through the action of walking.

Look for extra features such as removable footbed liners, breathable uppers and an Achilles notch. Ideally, you should choose a shoe that is designed specifically for the type of walking you enjoy — whether it's casual walking, brisk exercise walking or high-intensity aerobic walking.

## WALKING SHOE FEATURES

Look for the following key features for the best walking shoes:

(A)   MAXIMUM ARCH SUPPORT to provide proper support for arch; arch support should be soft, and with wear should form to your foot;

(B)   LOW MIDSOLE HEIGHT for proper cushioning and support. A walker requires a thinner midsole than a runner, due to less impact;

(C)   BEVELED HEEL to stabilize foot at heel strike;

(D)   FLEXIBLE FOREFRONT to offer comfort at toe raise and push-off;

(E)   FLAT TRACTION OUTSOLE for a more efficient stride during the "swing-through" phase of a walker's step, and;

(F)   PROPER FIT to provide comfort, support and protection with a wide, comfortable toe box and adequate width.

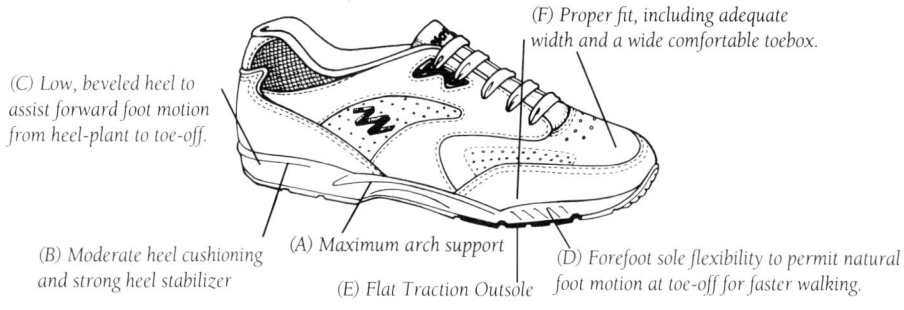

(C) Low, beveled heel to assist forward foot motion from heel-plant to toe-off.

(F) Proper fit, including adequate width and a wide comfortable toebox.

(B) Moderate heel cushioning and strong heel stabilizer

(A) Maximum arch support

(E) Flat Traction Outsole

(D) Forefoot sole flexibility to permit natural foot motion at toe-off for faster walking.

## FIVE POINTS TO REMEMBER
## WHEN BUYING A WALKING SHOE

Remember these five points when you buy your walking shoes:

1. Take your current pair of walking shoes with you to show wear patterns to the salesperson. This can identify your special needs.

2. Take along your favorite walking socks and try them on with the new shoes.

3. Try both right and left shoes on, then walk on a hard floor surface without carpeting.

4. Be aware of pressure areas, shoe friction, or slipping.

5. Allow time for the shoe to settle on your foot before you buy.

# STRETCHING: WARM UP BEFORE YOU WORK OUT

Adequate flexibility is essential to prevent injuries and soreness from walking. Take a few moments to stretch before you walk to increase your range of motion, enhance muscle relaxation, and alert your muscles that they are about to exercise. A quick stretching routine after a walk will create "muscle memory" to retain this new length for the next walking session.

## WHEN?
It is safer to stretch your muscles when they are warm. Warm-up can include 5-10 minutes of easy walking, or can be as simple as a few minutes of arm-swings, stair-climbing or even using a moist heat pack briefly before you stretch. When the muscles are warm and surging with blood, the tissues are more pliable.

## HOW?
A muscle must be relaxed before it can attain its maximum length. Focus on your technique, relaxing each muscle group by breathing deeply and slowly. By reducing tension in your muscles, your stretch will be centered in the bulk of the muscle and not on the surrounding ligaments and tendons, which should never be stretched. Be sensitive to your current level of flexibility in each muscle group. Don't push too hard or force the stretch. At the beginning of each stretch, inhale deeply, and exhale as you bend and flow into the stretch. Relax the stretch position, holding it for 20 seconds, while you visualize the gradual lengthening of your muscle. The only movement you make during each stretch will come from the steady rhythm of your slow, relaxed breathing.

## WHY?
Stretching promotes healthy, elastic muscles that are more resistant to muscle strains and sprains. To fully appreciate the benefits of stretching, be consistent. Stretch every day. Realize that your range of motion will depend on factors from prior days. For example, your calves may feel tight after a long, hilly walk taken the day before. Even if you experience tightness in any muscle group, a little stretching will remind your muscles of their ideal length. Remember, the benefit of stretching is much greater than flexibility. It helps both the mind and the body.

# STRETCHES

Use the following stretches to stay flexible and injury-free:

### #1 - HAMSTRING STRETCH

Lean forward from the waist, keeping your back straight and your chin parallel to your knees. Keep your abdomen tucked in. Stretch your left leg in this manner, keeping the right knee bent and tucked in to your left leg as shown. Hold 20 seconds. Repeat opposite side.

### #2 - HIP STRETCH

Use your right hand for support and keep your hip bones on the floor. Then tuck your right leg over the left leg at the knee and wrap your left arm around the right knee as shown. Hold 20 seconds. Repeat opposite side.

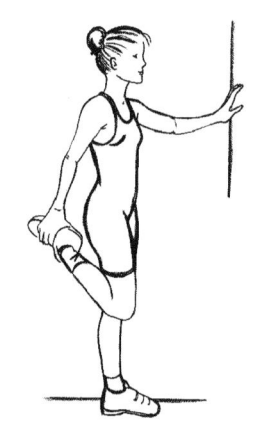

### #3 - QUADRICEP STRETCH

Hold a wall if necessary, and tuck your buttocks under and pull your right foot toward your buttocks as shown. Hold 20 seconds. Repeat opposite side.

### #4 - HIP FLEXOR STRETCH

With both legs forming 90° angles, touch the back knee to the floor. Rest your hands on the front knee. While keeping your back straight, tuck your hips under and forward. Hold 20 seconds. Repeat opposite side.

## #5 - INNER THIGH STRETCH

Sit on the floor, with your back straight, head up, eyes looking ahead, knees bent with the soles of your feet touching each other. Lean forward into the stretch. Hold 20 seconds. (Variation: Place your hands flat on the floor behind your buttocks; bring heels closer to body, then push your pelvis bones slightly off the floor while gently stretching your inner thigh.)

## #6 - SHOULDER STRETCH

Sit on the floor, with your back straight. Raise both arms overhead, reaching into a stretch. Keep your chin parallel to the floor and your shoulders relaxed. Imagine elongating your spine upward. Hold 20 seconds.

## #7 - CALF STRETCH

Stand next to a wall. Keeping your back knee straight, with the heel flat on the floor, lean into the wall, bending the opposite knee. Hold 20 seconds. Repeat opposite side.

# WALKING TECHNIQUE: HIGH-INTENSITY AEROBIC WALKING

Walking at any intensity will promote better fitness. But high-intensity aerobic walking is the exercise of choice to achieve a high level of cardiorespiratory endurance, and to burn calories at a greater rate. To walk at this intensity, you will want to develop a more efficient walking style. Use these guidelines to boost your walking workout intensity:

## POSTURE
Correct posture keeps you positioned to get the most power from your leg swing as you walk. Keep your foot close to the ground as you swing it forward with each step.

Begin by standing relaxed, with feet shoulder width apart. Lean forward from the ankles until you must step to keep from falling. This is a "5-degree forward body lean," which is the most efficient posture in walking.

Leaning too far backward results in high knee lift and weak arm action. Leaning too far forward causes you to land flat-footed, pulling your rear foot off the ground too soon.

## HEAD
Carry your head in a natural, relaxed position to keep your upper body loose. Focus your eyes on the ground a few yards ahead.

## TORSO
A relaxed upper body creates powerful coordinated body movements. Keep your shoulders horizontal (parallel) to the ground, squarely facing forward as your arms swing beneath them. Remember to keep your shoulders facing forward, without any movement or rotation front to back.

## ARMS
Use a powerful low and controlled arm swing for a more efficient stride. Carry your hands loosely, with palms facing inward and thumbs on top. Keep your thumb and elbow in a line, parallel to your waistband, to keep your shoulders low and in the correct position. Keep each elbow bent at a 90° angle. As you walk, drive your elbow straight back until the wrist meets the hip bone. Then, as your elbow swings forward, stop slightly in front of the hip. Avoid any side-to-side motion. As you bring your leading arm forward, your opposite leading leg will also swing forward. If you want to increase your pace, swing your arms faster and your legs will follow. Faster legs mean faster walking.

## HIPS

The hips are the power source of the walking movement. Increase your stride length and speed by increasing the action of your hips as you walk. Hip motion should be forward and backward. (A vertical stripe on the side seam of your shorts may help you to focus on the necessary hip rotation). Work toward a style of walking in which the hips direct your walking movement with strength and fluidity.

## LEGS & KNEES

When the hips are rotating properly, the low forward driving action of the knees will come naturally. Keep your knee joints relaxed. Straighten each leg as it passes under your body. By raising your toe at heel strike, the lower leg is slightly extended, straightening the knee.

## FEET

As your leg advances forward, your heel meets the ground first. Roll your foot gracefully, allowing it to flatten completely as it passes under your body. Keep the toe of your rear foot on the ground until the heel of your leading foot has made contact with the ground. Push off the rear foot with all your toes. Your toes should point forward to add extra length to your stride.

- Swing arms (bent at 90° angles) close to the body.

- Straighten knee as foot passes under hip.

- Keep 5° natural body lean from the ankle.

- Move hips front to back for power, speed and midsection toning.

- Land heel first, with toe up at a 40° angle from ground. Keep toes pointed forward.

# HEART RATE: LET YOUR HEART BE YOUR GUIDE

The wave of pressure flowing through your arteries with each heart beat is called your pulse or heart rate (HR). The pulse/HR is a safe guide to monitor your walking program. Pulse/HR can even determine a safe walking intensity and duration for the day.

Recommended heart rate levels listed here apply to healthy individuals with no cardiovascular or respiratory limitations. Before beginning any exercise program, consult your physician, especially if you are sedentary, overweight or over 35.

## FINDING YOUR PULSE/HR

Place your index and middle finger lightly on the thumbside of your wrist (radial artery) or on the right side of your neck near the Adam's apple (carotid artery). Because the thumb has a pulse of its own, always use the fingers, applying very light pressure (especially when checking the pulse via the carotid artery in the neck, as too much pressure in this area causes the heart to slow down).

Count the number of beats in one minute with the first beat being "zero." Record the rate and quality of the beats. Healthy or fit walkers will have a strong pulse, while illness or fatigue may create a weak pulse.

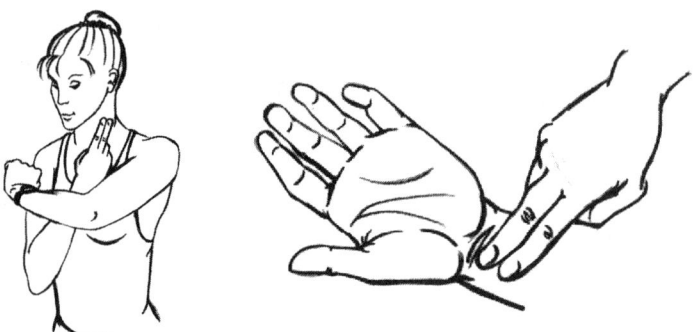

## RESTING HEART RATE (RHR)

The resting heart rate (or "basal pulse") is the number of heart beats per minute while the body is at the lowest activity level of the day or in a resting state. It is most accurately obtained when first waking in the morning, by taking the pulse for one minute before getting out of bed.

As your fitness increases, your RHR will decrease. By monitoring your RHR pattern over the course of weeks and months, you can be one step ahead of illness and injury.

## RECOVERY HEART RATE (R)

Your recovery rate is the rate at which your pulse returns to normal after walking. Take your pulse as soon as you finish walking, and again after one minute. After another minute has passed, take your pulse one more time. Walk slowly until your pulse drops to below 100 beats per minute (bpm). The faster your pulse recovers to a more normal rate, the more fit you are.

## MAXIMAL HEART RATE (MHR)

This is the highest heart rate a person can attain during heavy exercise. The most accurate method of determining your MHR is to obtain an exercise test with an electrocardiogram, taken in a controlled setting by trained specialists. A more convenient method of determining your MHR is to use the "Age-Predicted Heart Rate" formula: 220 - your age = your MHR. The figure 220 is the approximate MHR of a baby, which can vary +/- 10 bpm at any age. MHR generally decreases by one beat per year of age, which explains the reason for subtracting your age from 220 in this formula.

## TARGET HEART RATE (THR)

After you've achieved a slight sweat, take your pulse for 10 seconds, then multiply that pulse by 6 to see if you've reached your THR ZONE. When you are walking at your THR intensity, you should be sweating lightly and breathing harder. If, after taking your pulse, you find that you are walking below your THR, pick up your pace; if you are above your optimum THR range, relax and slow down.

Remember that each person's heart is individually influenced by many factors. Use these charts and zones as a guide. Always listen to your body.

# KARVONEN FORMULA
# (FOR DETERMINING TARGET HEART RATE)

|  | Sample | 60% | 70% |
|---|---|---|---|
| Begin here: | 220 | 220 | 220 |
| Subtract your age | -35 | -_____ | -_____ |
| Predicted maximum HR (MHR) | 163  185 | | |
| Subtract your resting HR (RHR) | -55 | -_____ | -_____ |
| Heart Rate Reserve | 130 | | |
| Multiply by intensity | x .60 | x .60 | x .70 |
|  | 78 | | |
| Add resting HR (RHR) | +55 | +_____ | +_____ |
| Target Heart Rate (THR) | 133 | _____ | _____ |
| Target Heart Rate Zone* | 133 to 146 | _____ | _____ |

\* It is best to determine a THR range or training zone. Accepted ranges for the Karvonen formula are 60-70% of heart rate reserve, plus resting heart rate. The Karvonen formula is an accurate way to determine THR, and is recommended by the American College of Sports Medicine.

# VISUALIZATION: WHAT YOU SEE IS WHAT YOU GET

Nothing has ever been achieved without first being conceived in the mind. Because about 85-90% of our exercise performance is mental, it is what's "upstairs" that counts! Follow these steps to use visualization to help you reach your fitness and personal goals:

## HOW TO BEGIN
Start with a goal — something you would like to achieve. It may be to have a trimmer body, to win a 5K race, or simply to feel more energy from your walk. Make your goal as specific as possible and write it down. Include as many details as you can and think about your goal often. Actually believe you can accomplish this goal that you've set for yourself. Your mind will soon accept these thoughts as reality.

## BREATHING
Abdominal or "belly" breathing is the way we gasped for our first breath of life. Babies unconsciously demonstrate this technique with superior skill. It is the most natural way to increase the volume of air inhaled with each breath. By its slow, expanding process, belly breathing allows life to slow down and become healthier. On each exhale of the belly breath, tensions are chased from the body.

Place one hand on your stomach and take a deep breath. As you inhale, feel your stomach rise. The upper abdomen fills with air, followed by the chest. As you exhale, let the air flow from your lungs at a comfortably slow rate. As you become more proficient, inhale through your nose, and exhale through your mouth, at a 1:2 ratio. For example, count to three as you breathe in, then count to six as you breathe out.

Begin every relaxation session with belly breathing. As you become more comfortable with the technique, incorporate belly breathing into your stretching and walking routines. The process gets easier with practice. Soon, this new, invigorating, form of breathing will replace the old habit of shallow chest-breathing.

## RELAXATION
The most effective visualization techniques occur while the body is in a calm state of relaxation. This alpha state is most like the "not fully awake but conscious" freshness of mind that is experienced when you first rise in the morning.

To reach a relaxed state, begin in a dark, quiet place where you will not be disturbed for 15 minutes. Sit or lie on the floor, progressively relaxing each and every part of your body. Greet each muscle with a soft "RELAX" until you feel a warm, calm, "letting-go" feeling. Use belly breathing to create a rhythm which quiets the mind and the body, creating overall relaxation. Slowly count backwards from 5 to 1, maintaining deep inhaling and exhaling on each number. Allow peace of mind to flow naturally.

## VISUALIZATION

Visualization is the process of rehearsing in your mind the successful outcome of a goal you wish to attain. The mind cannot tell the difference between an imagined experience and a real one. Therefore, when you take control of your thoughts, you take control of your unconscious mind — the master of your actions.

In the beginning stage of visualization, your mind will drift many times toward anything other than the visualization in progress. Relax and be patient; this is quite natural. Practice as often as possible. Allow at least one month of visualization exercises before you wish to achieve your goal.

## SAMPLE VISUALIZATION SESSION

In a relaxed state of mind, imagine yourself walking with perfect technique and smooth, fluid movements. Put yourself directly in the picture, seeing everything in the first person. What are you wearing? How do you look? You are in control of this "movie," so view yourself as the star, with the scene played in the present. Visualize as many details as possible. Experience effortless walking at your ideal body shape, and truly enjoy every step! Picture joyful interaction with other walkers and cheerful encouragement from onlookers. Smell the grass and leaves, and feel the breeze. Imagine the warmth of the sun on your neck and the cool sweat on your face as you get in touch with the feelings you wish to experience while walking. Say to yourself, "It feels easy and fun to walk three miles," and attach emotions to the words. Allow all of your senses to be involved with this perfect image of yourself.

Mental training will not guarantee success every time, but with practice, it will allow you to deal with your goals on a more personal level. By controlling your thoughts in a positive way through visualization, you will not leave to chance the success you desire in life, but empower yourself to achieve your goals. Your mind can become your best walking partner.

# NUTRITION:
# ENHANCE YOUR EXERCISE FROM THE INSIDE OUT

Athletes are continually seeking the ultimate aid to enhance their exercise routines. "What can I take to run faster, jump higher, and walk at the front of the pack?" High-energy bodies crave high-energy fuels to drive the body toward greatness. Healthy, nutritional "exercise enhancers" are foods, fluid replacements and supplements that allow you to gain energy and recover more quickly from each workout.

## COMPLEX CARBOHYDRATES

Complex carbohydrates provide the most efficient and cleanest-burning fuel for the body. They are the source of energy for muscle contraction, and are essential for fat metabolism. Complex carbohydrates boost energy and stamina. Some of the best sources are corn, potatoes, rice, pasta, whole grains, breads, and vegetables.

Complex carbohydrates are excellent sources of vitamins and minerals, which help keep your body functioning at an optimal level. As an added bonus, carbohydrates produce serotonin in the brain. Serotonin is a calm-inducing chemical that reduces tension.

Eating plenty of complex carbohydrates will train your body to store carbohydrates in the form of glycogen. Glycogen is a string of simple sugar molecules, released from the muscles and liver when you need extra fuel. Daily walks deplete your glycogen storage, so give your body an ample supply of complex carbohydrates each day to fully recover from your walks. Endurance walkers need at least 60% of total daily calories to come from complex carbohydrates.

Keep in mind that complex carbohydrates generally refer to foods that are natural, not chemically processed. Simple sugars do not offer the same healthy vitamins, minerals, water and fiber found in complex carbohydrates; eliminate sugary foods such as chocolate, cake, cookies, pie, doughnuts, soft drinks and candy from your diet.

## PROTEIN

Protein is essential for building and repairing muscles, red blood cells, hair and other tissues. When digested, protein breaks down into amino acids, which are then rebuilt into muscle and tissue protein. Approximately 15% of your daily calories should come from protein-rich foods, such as chicken, fish, beans or tofu.

## FATS

Dietary fats and oils can decrease the oxygen-carrying capacity of the blood and reduce a walker's endurance. Fat also slows the body's digestion process.

Although fat is necessary to convert carbohydrates to energy, it is un-necessary to add fat to your diet to gain its benefits. For optimal endurance and digestion, aim for no more than 25% of your daily calories to come from fat. Keep in mind that many common foods owe much of their calorie content to fat. New nutrition labeling on commercially prepared grocery items now requires that the product's fat content be listed, as well as what percentage of its calories are derived from fat. To make your choices easier, remember that only 25% of your daily calories should come from fat.

To find out the percentage of fat in a particular food, look for the number of grams of fat in the food, and multiply this number by 9 (each gram of fat has 9 calories). Take this number, and find the percentage of total calories which are fat by dividing it by the total calories.

Example: Chocolate candy pieces, 1 oz. (140 total calories, 6 grams of fat)

   6 (fat grams) x 9 (cal./fat gram) = 54 (fat calories)
   54 (fat calories) ÷ 140 (total calories) = approx. 38% fat

## FIBER

Walking exercises your "outsides," while fiber exercises your "insides." It is a vital part of everyone's diet — athlete and non-athlete. Good sources of fiber include beans, whole grains, fruits and vegetables. Generally, complex carbohydrates are rich in fiber. Target intake of fiber should be 25-35 grams a day. Remember to drink plenty of water when you eat a high-fiber diet to move the fiber out of your body.

# FLUIDS: WALKING ON WATER

The human body is amazing! Water, which makes up to 75% of your body, performs many important functions. From maintaining equilibrium to flushing toxins, water is precious to life. For the walking athlete, water can be considered a natural performance enhancer. It is commonly overlooked as a benefit to endurance, yet the loss of body fluids compromises the body's ability to circulate blood and regulate body temperature. As a walker becomes dehydrated, the heart rate increases and body temperature rises, making exercise labored.

## BEFORE THE WALK

Maximize your exercise benefit with water by water loading, or "hyperhydrating." The body's core temperature is lowered and the cardiovascular system works easier with extra water. Water loading also allows the body to sweat at an efficient rate throughout the walk. Sweat is necessary to cool the body: When you stop sweating, you should stop walking! A good rule of thumb for a longer walk or competition is to drink extra water for two days prior to the event and to follow this simple method of hyperhydrating the day of the walk:

1. 8 oz. every 10-15 minutes for 1-4 hours prior to the walk
2. 8 oz. 30 minutes prior to the walk
3. 8 oz. 20 minutes prior to the walk
   (Note: If you're exercising early in the morning, eliminate step 1.)

## DURING THE WALK

Drink one quart (8 oz. every 15 minutes) of water or a 5-10% carbohydrate solution for every hour you exercise. The best carbohydrate solution or replacement drinks (other than water) contain maltodextrin or glucose polymers, with a bit of fructose.

## AFTER THE WALK

After a longer walk or a walking competition, it's natural to be an "internal mess." Your stomach will be fairly empty and in a very acidic condition. Your muscles will be loaded with the metabolic waste products of exercise, and your glycogen "storage tank" will be empty. Finally, your body will be in a very dehydrated state, with a saturation of minerals floating throughout your system.

You may not feel thirsty, but the quickest recovery depends on immediate rehydration. Reach for a tall glass of cool water, then sip it slowly. Avoid citrus juices which add to the acidity in the stomach, and carbonated drinks which slow the rehydration process. Continue to drink extra water over the next 12 hours.

Adjust these suggestions according to your needs or intensity of your walk.

# WINTER WALKING: WEATHER OR NOT?

To many walkers, winter conjures visions of frosty fingers and numb toes, and exercise is put away with the summer clothing! Fortunately, you can enjoy exercise and improve your fitness by walking all year round. Keep the following in mind for winter walking:

### MYTHS AND FACTS ABOUT WINTER EXERCISE

**MYTH:** Your lungs might freeze when you exercise in cold temperatures.
**FACT:** Air inhaled at a temperature of -40° F, then tested in the mouth, shows a temperature of 50-60° F! It's actually quite safe to exercise outdoors on most winter days.

**MYTH::** Wearing gloves or mittens keeps your body warm.
**FACT:** When it's cold, your body conserves heat by taking it from your arms and legs to keep those internal organs warm. This ultimately causes a decrease in circulation at the extremities. Wearing gloves, mittens or even socks on your hands will keep them warm, but it's the layers of clothing worn on your torso that are the real key to staying warm in the winter.

**MYTH:** I don't need to wear a hat because my hair keeps my head warm in the winter.
**FACT:** Approximately 70% of your body heat is lost through your head and hands. The ears are prone to frostbite because of the surrounding air, so wear a hat for a more comfortable walk. Cover your face with a scarf, face mask or bandanna made from "winter-proof" materials when the temperature drops below 20° F.

**MYTH:** In the winter I don't need to drink as much water because I'm not sweating as much.
**FACT:** It may not seem true, but winter air (both outdoors and indoors) is very dry. In addition, each breath that you exhale releases moisture from your body. So, continue to drink extra water in the winter to nourish your skin.

**MYTH:** It's so cold in the winter that if I sweat I will freeze.
**FACT:** It is perfectly safe to perspire outdoors in the winter, provided you wear the right walking gear. Dress as though it were 10 degrees warmer than the thermometer shows, and layer your clothing. As your body warms up, heat will be generated within your walking suit, so wear mesh-vented linings and breathable outer items to let your body heat escape. Use removable sleeves, liners and hoods for versatility in cool and cold temperatures. Look for these man-made fabrics for warm, dry winter walking: Polypro®, Thermax®, Goretex®, Drylete®, Polartech®, Polar Lite® and Thermafleece®, and natural wool fabric. These synthetics, along with wool, retain body warmth while transferring moisture from the skin.

### ONE FINAL NOTE

Weight gain is more common in winter, perhaps because eating helps the body feel warmer. Exercise accomplishes this same warming effect without adding weight! If you just can't bear the cold, cross-train indoors with a treadmill, stationary bike, rowing machine or anything that gets the heart rate up and burns calories.

# STRENGTH: WEIGHT TRAINING AND DRILLS

## WEIGHT TRAINING

Walkers tend to overlook the weight room. Though walking does keep the body in fine shape, weight training improves muscle tone and increases the power of your walking stride. This, in turn, will help you achieve a faster and more efficient walking technique with less fatigue and injury.

To gain the most benefit from weight training, following a few basic principles correctly is more important than the type of equipment you use. Weight machines, free weights, dumbbells, even sand-filled milk jugs offer the resistance you want when weight training.

Weight training is best done consistently, every other day, with the day "off" designed as a period for recovery or rebuilding of your muscles. After generating a mild sweat, spend about 10 minutes stretching. Maintain proper form through three sessions ("sets") of 15 lifts ("reps") of each exercise. The greatest gains in your endurance come when you lift moderate weight for a higher number of reps. When you can easily accomplish three sets of 15 reps, you'll be ready to add another five pounds of weight to the exercise.

## EXERCISES

Use the following exercises to increase strength and tone:

### 1  BICEPS: BICEP CURLS

### 2  TRICEPS: ELBOW EXTENSIONS

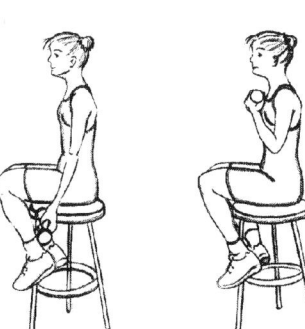
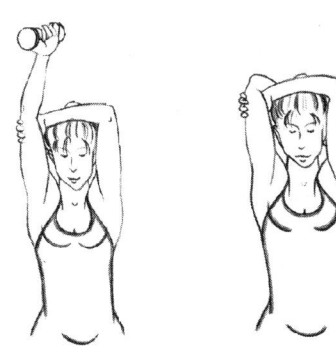

## 3  HAMSTRINGS: LEG CURLS

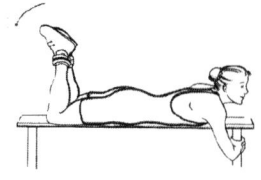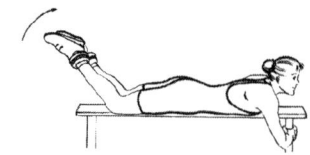

## 4  QUADRICEPS: LEG EXTENSIONS

## 5  CALVES: TOE RAISES
[Weight stays on shoulder. Raise up on your toes, then back down for one rep]

## 6  SHOULDERS/BACK: SEATED MILITARY

## 7  CHEST: BENCH PRESS

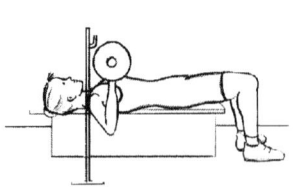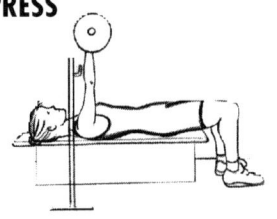

## 8  ABDOMEN: BENT KNEE SIT-UP    9  LOWER ABDOMEN: UNILATERAL LEG DROP

# DRILLS

The following simple exercise drills may seem peculiar or feel awkward, but they can be quite a lot of fun. Practice regularly to increase your flexibility and walking speed, while adding a spark to your workout program. Incorporate one or two drills each week into your walking sessions, and watch your walking attitude soar!

**SWEEPING:** While walking, clasp your hands in front of your body as if holding a baby. Twist the upper body to the right so your shoulders face sideways. Create a sweeping motion by pulling your left arm backwards as your right leg swings through. Alternate sides. (This drill helps you increase the length of your strides and improve your hip flexibility.)

**WINDMILL:** While walking, place the top of one wrist against the small of your back. With the other arm straight, begin swinging the arm backwards, making a full circle. Do this 15 times, then switch arms. Complete the drill by swinging both arms backwards (one at a time) while continuing to walk. Follow this with arm circles forward, one at a time. (This drill establishes upper body and lower body coordination.)

**HEELS/TOES:** Walk on your heels, with both legs straight at the knees and the toes pointed up as high as possible. Switch to landing on the toes while continuing to walk with straight legs. Do these heel and toe walks for 30 seconds each. (This drill strengthens the shins and stretches the hamstring muscles.)

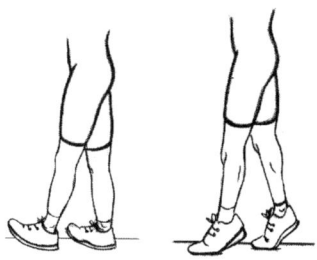

**CROSSWALK:** While walking on a straight line, begin crossing the line while maintaining good walking form. (This drill loosens the hips, buttocks, and outer legs.)

**FLOPPY ARMS:** Start with your arms straight at your side and very loose. Alternate rolling one shoulder, then the other, up to and back down from your earlobe. Let your arms totally relax and "flop." (This drill creates greater mobility in the torso and shoulders.)

# INJURY PREVENTION: INJURY-FREE WALKING

Walking is basically an injury-free exercise. Follow these simple guidelines to help keep your walking healthy and free of injury.

## FIVE FACTORS WHICH INFLUENCE THE CHANCE OF INJURY
Be aware of the following factors to limit your chance of injury:

## SURFACE
Walking on the same surface day after day with a sudden change to a different walking surface greatly increases the chance of injury—especially when coupled with any of the four factors listed below. When walking on a new surface, walk slower and shorter than usual.

## FOOTWEAR
Shoes not specifically designed for walking pose a threat to injury-free walking. Be certain that your shoes offer adequate comfort, support and protection.

## MINUTES/MILES
Gradually increase the amount of time that you walk each week (weekly mileage). Increase your weekly mileage no more than 10% from the prior week.

## INTENSITY
Walking at fast speeds puts great stress on your muscles and body. When incorporating a faster walk into your weekly program, always surround the effort with at least a day of easy walking, before and after the fast-walking day. This allows the muscles to be less fatigued for the fast-walking day, and provides more recovery the day after the intense walking session.

## TECHNIQUE
Practice good technique and proper body alignment to keep you walking injury-free.

## COMMON WALKING COMPLAINTS
Use the following list to identify and solve common walking complaints:

## COMPLAINT #1: "SHIN SPLINTS"
The shin muscles and tendons are designed to absorb shock with each step. If your shin is pushed to the point of fatigue and you feel an aching or stabbing pain, the muscle fibers of the shin may be swollen or slightly torn. The pain is often caused by walking too fast or too far for the condition of your shin muscles. An inward turning of the foot while walking (overpronation), increasing your walking mileage or walking on harder surfaces may also cause this condition.
**TIP:** Rub an ice cube up and down your shin until it feels numb, and elevate your legs. If the pain persists, see a podiatrist.

## COMPLAINT #2: "SORE FEET"
Pain on the bottom of your heel, especially when you raise up on your toes, is called plantar fasciitis. The plantar fascia is the band of connective tissue that supports the bottom of your foot — starting at the base of your five toes and going back along the bottom of your foot. Tight calf muscles put a great strain on the plantar fascia, so be certain to stay flexible through stretching. Overpronation is also a factor in some cases; it causes the toes to move forward, overstretching the plantar fascia.
**TIP:** Add an arch support to your shoes to limit excessive arch stretch and movement within your shoe. If the pain persists, see a podiatrist.

## COMPLAINT #3: "HIP PAIN"
The iliotibial (IT) band is a band of connective tissue which runs along your outer thigh from hip to knee. It is at work as you straighten your knee while walking. Generally, tightness felt at your hip or outer knee joint is caused by increased mileage or a biomechanical foot abnormality.
**TIP:** Use ice to reduce inflammation at the site of pain. Use the hip stretch as good preventive medicine (see the section on STRETCHING in this guide).

# GLOSSARY
Refer to this list of terms and their definitions as additional background:
**LIGAMENTS:** Tough, fibrous tissue connecting bone to bone
**ORTHOTICS:** Molded arch supports to help align the feet
**SPRAIN:** Irritation, slight swelling, or microscopic tearing of ligaments
**STRAIN:** Irritation, slight swelling, or microscopic tearing of muscles or tendons
**TENDON:** Tough, fibrous tissue connecting muscle to bone
**TENDINITIS:** Irritated, swollen or strained tendon

# BODY SCULPTURING: WEIGHT LOSS THROUGH FAT LOSS

## BODY IMAGE

Create your body as you would most desire it. Use your imagination, an old photograph or a picture from a magazine. This ideal shape is your goal. So put the picture in a place where you will see it daily — on a wall, the refrigerator, or in your walk log. This visual reminder will send your brain a sculptured map of your body at its finest.

To facilitate results, replace negative self-talk with affirmations. These are positive words or statements that guide your thoughts on a more productive path. Refer to the following list of sample affirmations and tips to begin the reprogramming process in your brain.

## AFFIRMATIONS
- I only desire foods that give me energy and contribute to my fat-burning body.
- I enjoy walking, and the toned, lean feeling it creates in my legs and buttocks.
- I deserve to have a slender, fat-free body.

## PARTY SECRETS
- Offer to bring fruit, vegetables, salad or whole grain snack muffins to a gathering.
- Before leaving for a social event, drink a glass of vegetable juice, fresh orange or grapefruit juice, or even plain water as a healthy appetite suppressant.
- Eat the larger holiday meal at noon, and prepare a "leftover plate" for dinner snacking.

## RESTAURANT SECRETS
- Order condiments, dressings and sauces on the side.
- Sip on ice-free lemon water while waiting to be served.
- Say "no" to desserts — or try a fruit cup instead.
- Avoid fried foods — stick to grilled, baked, steamed or poached items.

## TRAVEL SECRETS
- Always have a healthy snack bar, fruit or vegetable in your purse or briefcase.
- Enjoy sightseeing on foot, rather than in a car
- Take advantage of fitness facilities found at many hotels and resorts
- Ask your hotel desk clerk or concierge about safe walking routes near the hotel

## EXERCISE SECRETS

- Use aerobic walking at a continuous but moderately low intensity as the quickest way to burn fat.
- Fat cells fuel the muscles with energy. Walking on an empty stomach encourages the muscles (instead of fat cells) to be used as fuel. Feed your body a small amount of carbohydrate before you walk, such as an apple, slice of bread or carbo-drink.
- A consistent program of walking is an excellent way to burn calories and fat. But keep in mind that by adding extra exercise — like taking the stairs at work, or walking instead of driving whenever possible — you'll burn extra calories and feel more energetic.

## PRIDE

Women generally maintain a higher level of fat cells than men, and their skin is thinner and more delicate. In addition, the fat beneath a woman's skin forms large, round overfilled cells, while a man's fat cell compartments are sectioned into small units that do not bulge when filled. Finally, female hormones encourage a higher percentage of body fat than do male hormones. Fortunately, with proper diet and exercise, women can reduce their body fat and gain a sleeker, healthier body.

Take pride in the fact that you are a woman, and smile when you look in the mirror. ACT as though you are already at YOUR "perfect" shape. View yourself in a full-length mirror often to get a better overall assessment of your progress. Gradually bring the once "tight-fitting" clothing closer and closer to the front of your closet. Compliments from family and friends are inevitable as you get nearer and nearer to your ideal body image. While these compliments will certainly make you feel better, the compliments you give directly to yourself are the most valuable to your self-esteem!

## BE PATIENT!

According to psychologists, it takes about 21 days to make or break any habit. Be patient. In just three weeks, you can be completely on your way toward beating the poor nutrition habit by replacing old ways of eating with new, healthy, balanced eating habits. Use the fat loss tips listed here in combination with a consistent walking program, and watch the fat burn from your body.

# SAMPLE WALKING PROGRAM

A sample schedule is given here for each of the three levels of walking — (1) CASUAL WALKING, (2) BRISK EXERCISE WALKING, AND (3) AEROBIC WALKING. Choose the program which best resembles your fitness ability, and use the sample sessions as a guideline. Remember to listen to YOUR body.

## CASUAL WALKER

Description: Walks at an easy, relaxed pace for enjoyment or light exercise, typically at a casual 18-30 minutes-per-mile pace.

| Week | Day 1 | Day 2 | Day 3 | Day 4 | Day 5 | Day 6 | Day 7 |
|------|-------|-------|-------|-------|-------|-------|-------|
| 1 | 20 min. | Rest | 25 min. | Rest | 20 min | Rest | 20 min. |
| 2 | Rest | 25 min. | 20 min. | Rest | 25 min. | Rest | 25 min. |
| 3 | 20 min. | 25 min. | Rest | 30 min. | Rest | 25 min. | 20 min. |
| 4 | Rest | 30 min. | 20 min. | 25 min. | Rest | 30 min. | 25 min. |
| 5 | 30 min. | Rest | 20 min. | 30 min. | 25 min. | Rest | 20 min. |
| 6 | 25 min. | 30 min. | Rest | 30 min. | 25 min. | Rest | 30 min. |

1 mile = 1.60934 km

## BRISK WALKER

Description: Walks regularly at a brisk pace for a challenging workout, usually at a quick 14-17 minutes-per-mile pace.

| Week | Day 1 | Day 2 | Day 3 | Day 4 | Day 5 | Day 6 | Day 7 |
|---|---|---|---|---|---|---|---|
| 1 | 45 min. | Rest | 45 min. | 45 min. | 40 min. | Rest | 50 min. |
| 2 | Rest | 45 min. | 40 min. | 45 min. | Rest | 50 min. | 40 min. |
| 3 | 45 min. | Rest | 45 min. | 45 min. | Rest | 40 min. | 50 min. |
| 4 | Rest | 45 min. | 45 min. | 50 min. | 40 min. | Rest | 45 min. |
| 5 | 45 min. | 40 min. | 50 min. | Rest | 45 min. | Rest | 45 min. |
| 6 | 45 min. | 40 min. | Rest | 50 min. | Rest | 45 min. | 45 min. |

## AEROBIC WALKER

Description: Walks regularly at an accelerated pace to attain the highest level of aerobic fitness, usually at an intense 10-13 minutes-per-mile pace.

| Week | Day 1 | Day 2 | Day 3 | Day 4 | Day 5 | Day 6 | Day 7 |
|---|---|---|---|---|---|---|---|
| 1 | 1 hr. | Rest | 45 min.* | 30 min. | 1 hr. | 30 min. | 45 min. |
| 2 | Rest | 1 hr. | 30 min. | 45 min.* | 30 min. | 1 hr. | 45 min. |
| 3 | 30 min. | Rest | 45 min.* | 30 min. | 1 hr. | 30 min. | 45 min. |
| 4 | 1 hr. | 30 min. | 45 min. | Rest | 45 min.* | 30 min. | 1 hr. |
| 5 | 45 min. | Rest | 1 hr. | 30 min. | 1 hr. | 45 min. | 30 min. |
| 6 | Rest | 1 hr. | 30 min. | 45 min.* | 30 min. | 45 min. | 1 hr. |

* = A more challenging pace for one-third of the workout time, generally in the middle of the walk.

# COMMONLY ASKED QUESTIONS ON WALKING

## IS IT BETTER TO WALK FOR DISTANCE OR SPEED?
These two types of training methods can be mixed into your walking schedule to keep your muscles fresh. Each training method has a different benefit, yet both are intensely demanding on the body. One becomes the focus, and the other adds a splash of variety. If your fitness objective is to lose weight and develop muscular endurance, a greater percentage of your weekly mileage will be longer walks. If your goal is a competition or raising your cardiovascular fitness level, speed will become important. Remember, with regard to speed, more is not always better.

## MY FRIEND AND I ENJOY WALKING TOGETHER, BUT WE ARE NOT TRAINING AT THE SAME PACE. WHAT CAN WE DO?
Walking programs are best when individually based on heart rate. However, walking with a partner is a great way to stay motivated. One method is to begin your walk together, and walk a familiar course. The faster walker finishes the course and then walks back to meet her friend. Both can then finish together. Taking side streets can work for the faster walker, too, while the other walker stays straight on the course. Walking an outdoor track, the slower walker may walk in lane one and the faster walker may walk in either lane three or four. Another alternative is to seek a fitness club with two side-by-side treadmills.

## IS SHOPPING WALKING?
Unfortunately, a leisurely stroll down the supermarket aisles does not count as aerobic walking. Walking is effective as exercise when you walk briskly for at least 20 minutes. Exercise that requires deeper, faster inhaling and exhaling of air in to the lungs increases the body's use of oxygen, and is referred to as an aerobic ("with air") exercise. To be classified as "casual walking," the walker's pace should be no slower than 30 minutes per mile.

## WHAT CAN I DO TO ELIMINATE SHIN SPLINTS WHEN I WALK?
"Shin splints" is a catchall term to describe the pain felt along the shin bone (tibia). For mild pain, massage the area for five minutes with a single ice cube after your walk. If you feel pain during the walk, take a moment to stop and stand on the toes for 30 seconds. This relaxes the shin by contracting the calf muscle. Continue the walk with a lower toe angle until your shin muscles become stronger.

## HOW MANY CALORIES DO I BURN WHEN I WALK?

Calories "burned" depend on distance, body weight and speed.

*Calories Burned Per Minute*

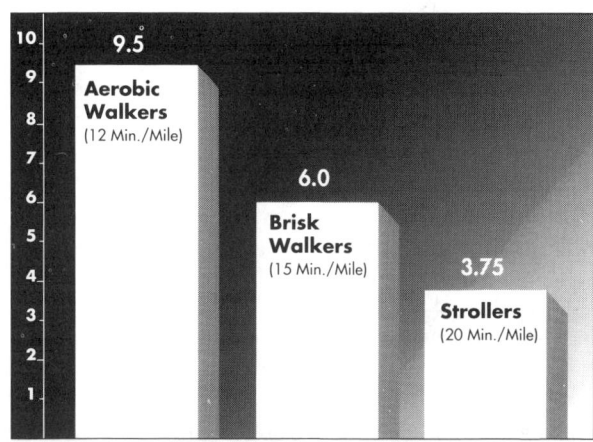

Walking Pace (minutes per mile)

## IS IT NECESSARY TO WEAR SOCKS?
Socks provide protection for your feet and your shoes. Even under normal conditions, each foot gives off about one cup of perspiration a day. This moisture encourages blisters, and because it is slightly acidic, it can also cause the lining of your shoes to break down prematurely.

## WHAT CAN I DO ABOUT LEG CRAMPS?
Cramping can be a sign of fatigue or dehydration. However, if the soreness you feel is a cramp of the muscle, the best way to relax it is to contract the opposite muscle group: For example, if the cramp you feel is in the back of your thighs (hamstrings), you should contract the muscles in the front of your thighs (quadriceps) until the hamstring cramp subsides. For a calf cramp, pull the toes up to contract the shin muscles.

## HOW CAN I KEEP MY WORKOUTS INTERESTING?
The first few walking sessions will be exciting because you will see quick progress. After a couple of weeks, it may be time to alternate routes or walk with a partner. Music is a great way to pass the time if exercise becomes mundane, but use good sense when wearing headphones outdoors.

# IS WALKING BETTER THAN RUNNING?

The NaturalSport Walking Study conducted at the Cooper Institute for Aerobics Research showed that walking at any pace can improve your fitness level and reduce your risk of coronary heart disease...and that brisk or aerobic walking can multiply these fitness benefits and help you lose weight without threat of injury. <u>Women who walked at a pace of 12-15 minutes per mile increased their cardiorespiratory fitness as well as runners, but with far less risk of orthopedic injury.</u>

The heart cannot distinguish between walking or running, and both exercises utilize a great amount of muscle mass. In fact, aerobic walking demands the involvement of more muscle groups than running. Walking at a pace of 12 minutes per mile or faster actually burns more calories and provides a more intense workout than running at that same pace. And since a walker keeps one foot on the ground at all times, she withstands less impact than a runner, places less stress on her skeletal system, and lowers her risk of injury. Overall, walking is an exercise that will provide you with the same or better fitness benefits as running, but with a much lower risk of injury. Consult your doctor before starting any exercise program. The NaturalSport Walking Study revealed the benefits associated with walking at three intensity levels:

## AEROBIC WALKING
Women who walked an average pace of 12 minutes per mile achieved the cardiorespiratory fitness improvements of runners, and burned more than twice as many calories as casual walkers. Average calorie expenditure for aerobic walking is 9.5 calories per minute.
**Intensity:** 10-13 minutes per mile.
**Frequency:** Recommended minimum of four days a week.
**Duration:** Goal is to achieve three miles per walk.

## BRISK WALKING
Brisk exercise walkers improved their fitness levels by 9%, increased their cardiorespiratory capacity and burned more calories than casual walkers. Average calorie expenditure for brisk walking is 6 calories per minute.
**Intensity:** 14-17 minutes per mile.
**Frequency:** Recommended minimum of three to four days a week.
**Duration:** Goal is to achieve three miles per walk.

## CASUAL WALKING
Women who walk regularly at a casual pace or stroll increased their cardiorespiratory fitness while decreasing their risk of heart disease. Average calorie expenditure for casual walking is 4 calories per minute.
**Intensity:** 18-30 minutes per mile.
**Frequency:** Recommended minimum of three days a week. Slower walkers should consider walking more frequently, up to five or six days a week.
**Duration:** Goal is to achieve three miles per walk.

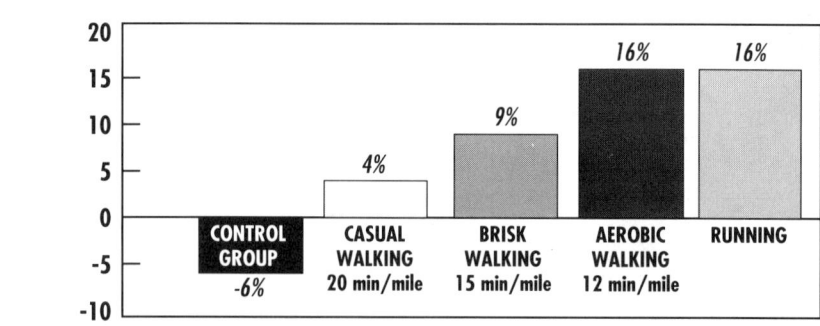

*As measured by maximum oxygen uptake. Source: NaturalSport Walking Study, Institute for Aerobics Research, Dallas, Texas.

# YOUR PERSONAL WALKING LOG

Note the following helpful information in your new walking log. Additionally, each day record anything which affects you in reaching your goal.

## SHOES
Make a note of your walking shoes. This is a great reference when you want to find out how many miles/months your shoe lasts under your specific weight, gait and mileage.

## COURSE — WEATHER — TIME OF DAY
Was the route hilly, flat, on gravel or on a track? Was it hot, sunny, cool, rainy, snowy, icy, shaded? Did you walk early in the morning, at high noon, in the dark or after dinner?

## PARTNER
Did you walk alone or with a partner? Sometimes a walking companion is good for your walk, forcing you to keep up the pace and feeding your competitive streak. Other times a walking companion is a distraction to your exercise goal for the day. Note your feelings, and match these to your walking pace, heart rate, miles/minutes and attitude about the walk that day.

## BASAL PULSE
This is a very accurate indicator of your recovery from the last exercise session, or from any stresses from the prior day. Take your pulse just before you get out of bed. Note the number, and adjust your walking routine for the day accordingly. Any deviation of 5 or more beats from the previous day signals a need for an easier day of exercise.

## MORNING WEIGHT
This can be helpful if taken on a regular basis, just out of bed and right after elimination. Major decreases in weight from day to day may denote dehydration. As your body shape gets closer to your ideal, expect your weight to stabilize or possibly increase slightly over many months. This is natural, as the muscles you develop weigh more than the fat you lose. However, your body will be toned, and your body fat percentage will be lower.

## HEART RATE

Note your heart rate during each walk, and your recovery heart rate after you finish (review Heart Rate Section). Enjoy seeing your progress as you become more fit, and be aware of how your body handles each walk.

## MILEAGE — MINUTES — PACE

Note the total exercise time, the total distance walked, the pace at which you covered the distance, or all of these. Don't become obsessed with the amount of distance you can cover in a specific time each day. A distance "test" is beneficial once a week or once every two weeks.

## FOOD/WATER INTAKE

Briefly list foods eaten during the day. Look back on what was eaten to help you assess your energy (or lack of it) in the days that follow.

## DAILY STRESSES, ILLNESSES OR INJURIES

Record any factors that may have caused a justified "day off" from walking, or anything that may have made the walk a much-needed release for the day. Include travel, meeting deadlines, hours slept (too few or too many) or even a day of errands. These all drain your daily energy reserves.

Fill in all the days, even those that did not include exercise. On "off days," just draw a big "zero" on the particular day and state the reason: non-training day, too busy, ill, leg pains, etc. By keeping to a consistent exercise pattern (every other day, M-W-F, daily), the routine will become a hard habit to break.

One final note: Keep the "days off" to no more than three consecutive days. More than three days not exercising tends to negate the progress you have made. Have fun and enjoy your walk!

# MEASUREMENTS: HOW DO YOU MEASURE UP?

After beginning your walking program, take your measurements once a month, at the same time of day each month (i.e., before breakfast). As you increase your fitness level, you will see an improvement in your measurements which may not be reflected on the scale. Because muscle weighs more than fat, you may even gain a pound or two as you lose body fat and gain muscle. Don't let the scale be your ruler! It is far better to check your measurements instead, for they are a more accurate indicator of your progress. Use the following charts to note your measurements.

*Tape a photo*

*of your ideal body here*

*(use a personal photo*

*or a picture from a magazine).*

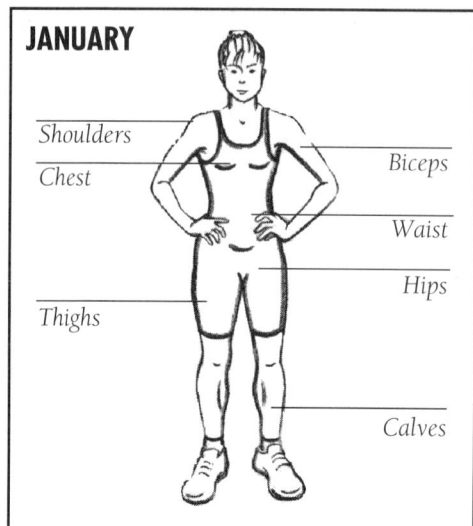
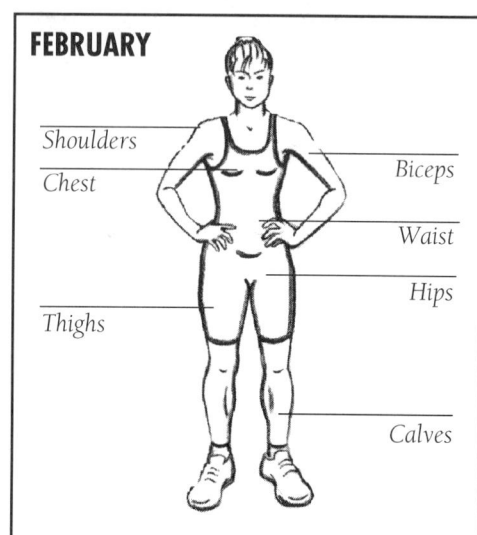
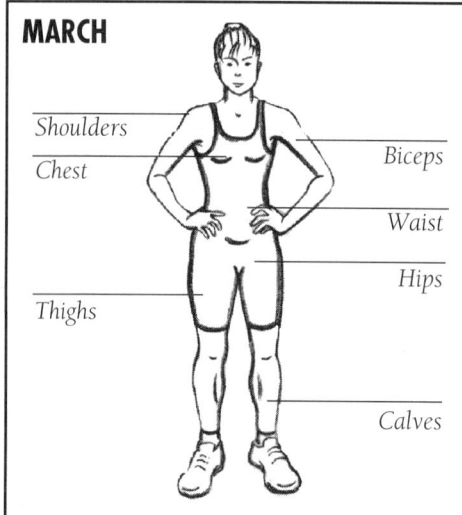
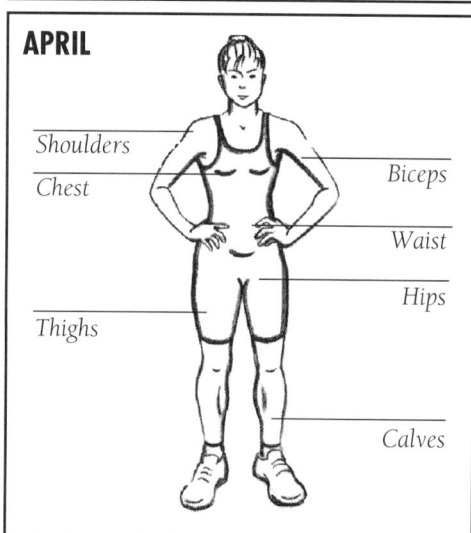
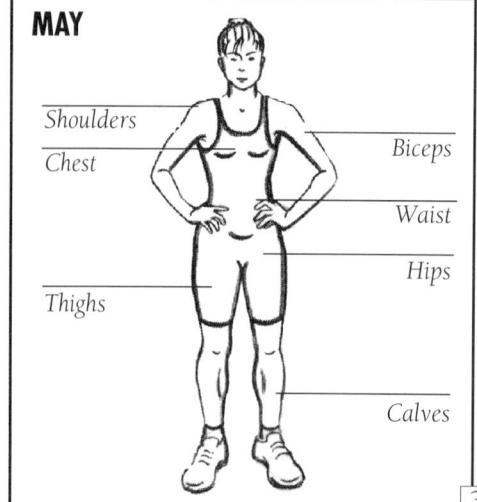
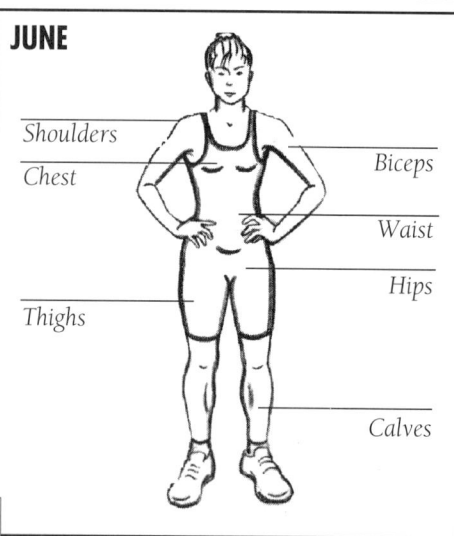

## JULY

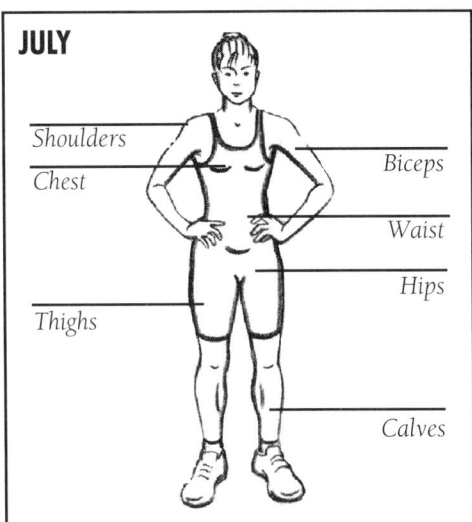

- Shoulders
- Chest
- Biceps
- Waist
- Hips
- Thighs
- Calves

## AUGUST

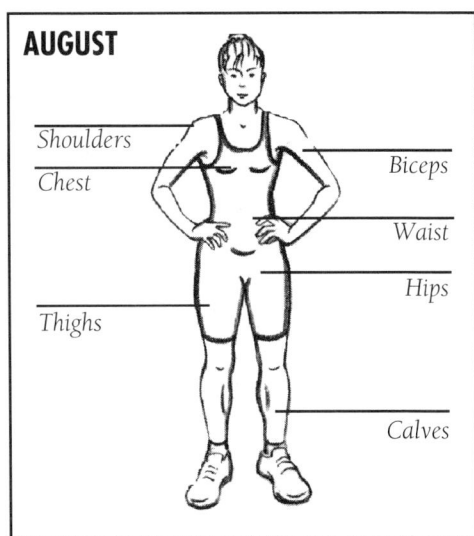

- Shoulders
- Chest
- Biceps
- Waist
- Hips
- Thighs
- Calves

## SEPTEMBER

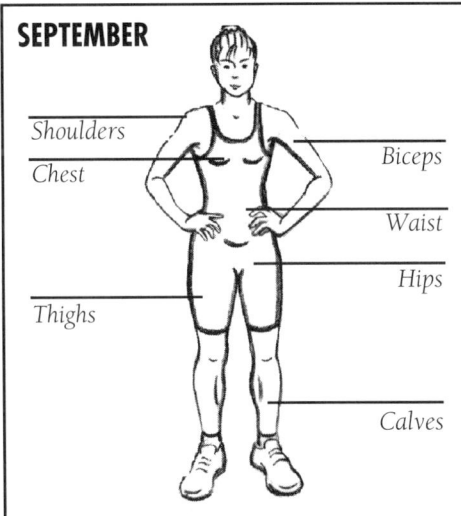

- Shoulders
- Chest
- Biceps
- Waist
- Hips
- Thighs
- Calves

## OCTOBER

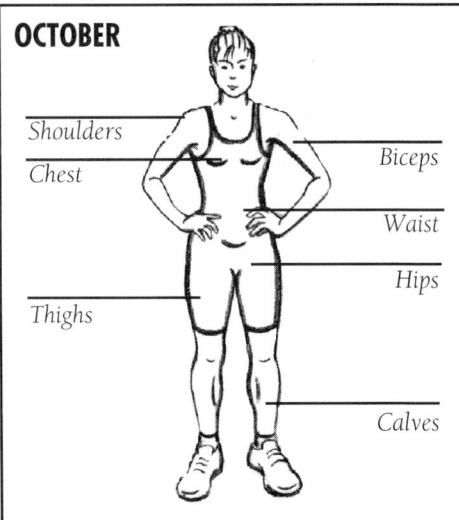

- Shoulders
- Chest
- Biceps
- Waist
- Hips
- Thighs
- Calves

## NOVEMBER

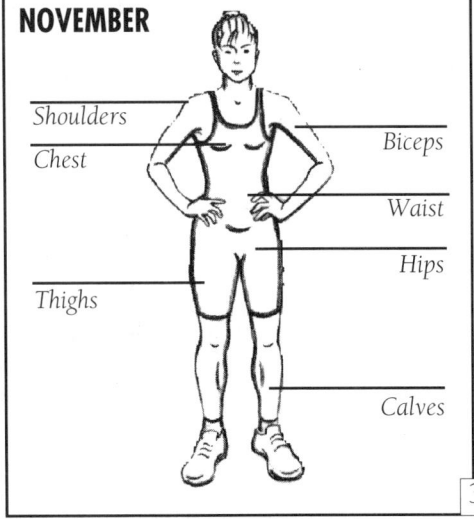

- Shoulders
- Chest
- Biceps
- Waist
- Hips
- Thighs
- Calves

## DECEMBER

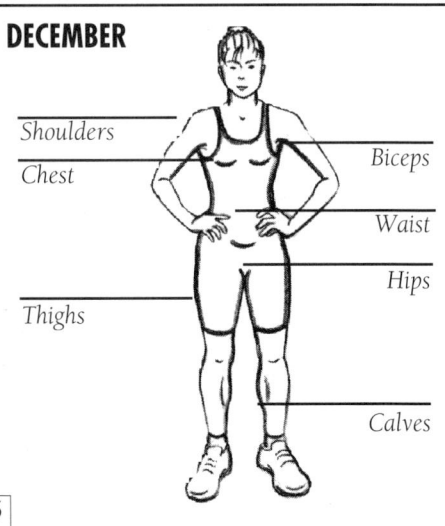

- Shoulders
- Chest
- Biceps
- Waist
- Hips
- Thighs
- Calves

# WEEKLY MILEAGE AT A GLANCE

| WEEK | Mon. | Tue. | Wed. | Thu. | Fri. | Sat. | Sun. | TOTAL |
|---|---|---|---|---|---|---|---|---|
| | | | | | | | | |
| | | | | | | | | |
| | | | | | | | | |
| | | | | | | | | |
| | | | | | | | | |
| | | | | | | | | |
| | | | | | | | | |
| | | | | | | | | |
| | | | | | | | | |
| | | | | | | | | |
| | | | | | | | | |
| | | | | | | | | |
| | | | | | | | | |
| | | | | | | | | |
| | | | | | | | | |
| | | | | | | | | |
| | | | | | | | | |
| | | | | | | | | |
| | | | | | | | | |
| | | | | | | | | |
| | | | | | | | | |
| | | | | | | | | |
| | | | | | | | | |
| | | | | | | | | |
| | | | | | | | | |
| | | | | | | | | |

# WEEKLY MILEAGE AT A GLANCE

| WEEK | Mon. | Tue. | Wed. | Thu. | Fri. | Sat. | Sun. | TOTAL |
|------|------|------|------|------|------|------|------|-------|
|      |      |      |      |      |      |      |      |       |
|      |      |      |      |      |      |      |      |       |
|      |      |      |      |      |      |      |      |       |
|      |      |      |      |      |      |      |      |       |
|      |      |      |      |      |      |      |      |       |
|      |      |      |      |      |      |      |      |       |
|      |      |      |      |      |      |      |      |       |
|      |      |      |      |      |      |      |      |       |
|      |      |      |      |      |      |      |      |       |
|      |      |      |      |      |      |      |      |       |
|      |      |      |      |      |      |      |      |       |
|      |      |      |      |      |      |      |      |       |
|      |      |      |      |      |      |      |      |       |
|      |      |      |      |      |      |      |      |       |
|      |      |      |      |      |      |      |      |       |
|      |      |      |      |      |      |      |      |       |
|      |      |      |      |      |      |      |      |       |
|      |      |      |      |      |      |      |      |       |
|      |      |      |      |      |      |      |      |       |
|      |      |      |      |      |      |      |      |       |
|      |      |      |      |      |      |      |      |       |
|      |      |      |      |      |      |      |      |       |
|      |      |      |      |      |      |      |      |       |
|      |      |      |      |      |      |      |      |       |
|      |      |      |      |      |      |      |      |       |
|      |      |      |      |      |      |      |      |       |
|      |      |      |      |      |      |      |      |       |
|      |      |      |      |      |      |      |      |       |
|      |      |      |      |      |      |      |      |       |
|      |      |      |      |      |      |      |      |       |

# PACE CHART

*k=Kilometers   m=Meters   mi=Miles*

| Pace/mi | 400m<br>Track Laps: 1<br>.25mi | 1k<br>2.5<br>0.6mi | 3k<br>7.5<br>1.8mi | 5k<br>12.5<br>3.1mi | 10k<br>25<br>6.2mi | 15k<br>37.5<br>9.3mi | 20k<br>50<br>20.4mi | 42k<br>105<br>26.2mi | 50k<br>125<br>31.1mi |
|---|---|---|---|---|---|---|---|---|---|
| 6:00 | 1:30 | 3:44 | 11:11 | 18:38 | 37:17 | 55:55 | 1:14:34 | 2:37:12 | 3:06:25 |
| 6:10 | 1:32 | 3:50 | 11:30 | 19:10 | 38:19 | 57:29 | 1:16:38 | 2:41:34 | 3:11:35 |
| 6:20 | 1:35 | 3:56 | 11:48 | 19:41 | 39:21 | 59:02 | 1:18:42 | 2:45:56 | 3:16:46 |
| 6:30 | 1:38 | 4:02 | 12:07 | 20:12 | 40:23 | 1:00:35 | 1:20:47 | 2:50:18 | 3:21:57 |
| 6:40 | 1:40 | 4:09 | 12:26 | 20:43 | 41:25 | 1:02:08 | 1:22:51 | 2:54:40 | 3:27:07 |
| 6:50 | 1:42 | 4:15 | 12:44 | 21:14 | 42:28 | 1:03:41 | 1:24:55 | 2:59:02 | 3:32:18 |
| 7:00 | 1:45 | 4:21 | 13:03 | 21:45 | 43:30 | 1:05:15 | 1:27:00 | 3:03:24 | 3:37:29 |
| 7:10 | 1:48 | 4:27 | 13:22 | 22:16 | 44:32 | 1:06:48 | 1:29:04 | 3:07:46 | 3:42:39 |
| 7:20 | 1:50 | 4:33 | 13:40 | 22:47 | 45:34 | 1:08:21 | 1:31:08 | 3:12:08 | 3:47:50 |
| 7:30 | 1:52 | 4:40 | 13:59 | 23:18 | 46:36 | 1:09:54 | 1:33:12 | 3:16:30 | 3:53:01 |
| 7:40 | 1:55 | 4:46 | 14:17 | 23:49 | 47:38 | 1:11:27 | 1:35:17 | 3:20:52 | 3:58:12 |
| 7:50 | 1:58 | 4:52 | 14:36 | 24:20 | 48:40 | 1:13:01 | 1:37:21 | 3:25:14 | 4:03:22 |
| 8:00 | 2:00 | 4:58 | 14:55 | 24:51 | 49:43 | 1:14:34 | 1:39:25 | 3:29:36 | 4:08:38 |
| 8:10 | 2:02 | 5:04 | 15:13 | 25:22 | 50:45 | 1:16:07 | 1:41:29 | 3:33:58 | 4:13:44 |
| 8:20 | 2:05 | 5:11 | 15:32 | 25:53 | 51:47 | 1:17:40 | 1:43:34 | 3:38:20 | 4:18:54 |
| 8:30 | 2:08 | 5:17 | 15:51 | 26:24 | 52:49 | 1:19:13 | 1:45:38 | 3:42:42 | 4:24:05 |
| 8:40 | 2:10 | 5:23 | 16:09 | 26:56 | 53:51 | 1:20:47 | 1:47:42 | 3:47:04 | 4:29:16 |
| 8:50 | 2:12 | 5:29 | 16:28 | 27:27 | 54:53 | 1:22:20 | 1:49:47 | 3:51:26 | 4:34:26 |
| 9:00 | 2:15 | 5:36 | 16:47 | 27:58 | 55:55 | 1:23:53 | 1:51:51 | 3:55:48 | 4:39:37 |
| 9:10 | 2:18 | 5:42 | 17:05 | 28:29 | 56:58 | 1:25:26 | 1:53:55 | 4:00:10 | 4:44:48 |
| 9:20 | 2:20 | 5:48 | 17:24 | 29:00 | 58:00 | 1:27:00 | 1:55:59 | 4:04:32 | 4:49:58 |
| 9:30 | 2:22 | 5:54 | 17:43 | 29:31 | 59:02 | 1:28:33 | 1:58:04 | 4:08:54 | 4:55:09 |
| 9:40 | 2:25 | 6:00 | 18:01 | 30:02 | 1:00:04 | 1:30:06 | 2:00:08 | 4:13:16 | 5:00:20 |
| 9:50 | 2:28 | 6:07 | 18:20 | 30:33 | 1:01:06 | 1:31:39 | 2:02:12 | 4:17:38 | 5:05:30 |
| 10:00 | 2:30 | 6:13 | 18:38 | 31:04 | 1:02:08 | 1:33:12 | 2:04:16 | 4:22:00 | 5:10:41 |
| 10:30 | 2:38 | 6:31 | 19:34 | 32:37 | 1:05:15 | 1:37:52 | 2:10:29 | 4:35:06 | 5:26:13 |
| 11:00 | 2:45 | 6:50 | 20:30 | 34:11 | 1:08:21 | 1:42:32 | 2:16:42 | 4:48:12 | 5:41:45 |
| 11:30 | 2:52 | 7:09 | 21:26 | 35:44 | 1:11:27 | 1:47:11 | 2:22:55 | 5:01:18 | 5:57:17 |
| 12:00 | 3:00 | 7:27 | 22:22 | 37:17 | 1:14:34 | 1:51:51 | 2:29:08 | 5:14:24 | 6:12:49 |
| 12:30 | 3:08 | 7:46 | 23:18 | 38:50 | 1:17:40 | 1:56:30 | 2:35:21 | 5:27:30 | 6:28:21 |
| 13:00 | 3:15 | 8:05 | 24:14 | 40:23 | 1:20:47 | 2:01:10 | 2:41:33 | 5:40:36 | 6:43:53 |
| 13:30 | 3:22 | 8:23 | 25:10 | 41:57 | 1:23:53 | 2:05:50 | 2:47:46 | 5:53:42 | 6:59:26 |
| 14:00 | 3:30 | 8:42 | 26:06 | 43:30 | 1:27:00 | 2:10:29 | 2:53:59 | 6:06:48 | 7:14:58 |
| 14:30 | 3:38 | 9:01 | 27:02 | 45:03 | 1:30:06 | 2:15:09 | 3:00:12 | 6:19:54 | 7:30:30 |
| 15:00 | 3:45 | 9:19 | 27:58 | 46:36 | 1:33:12 | 2:19:49 | 3:06:25 | 6:33:00 | 7:46:02 |
| 15:30 | 3:52 | 9:38 | 28:54 | 48:09 | 1:36:19 | 2:24:28 | 3:12:38 | 6:46:06 | 8:01:34 |
| 16:00 | 4:00 | 9:57 | 29:50 | 49:43 | 1:39:25 | 2:29:08 | 3:18:50 | 6:59:12 | 8:17:06 |
| 16:30 | 4:08 | 10:15 | 30:45 | 51:16 | 1:42:32 | 2:33:47 | 3:25:03 | 7:12:18 | 8:32:38 |
| 17:00 | 4:15 | 10:34 | 31:41 | 52:49 | 1:45:38 | 2:38:27 | 3:31:16 | 7:25:24 | 8:48:10 |
| 17:30 | 4:22 | 10:52 | 32:37 | 54:22 | 1:48:44 | 2:43:07 | 3:37:29 | 7:38:30 | 9:03:42 |
| 18:00 | 4:30 | 11:11 | 33:33 | 55:55 | 1:51:51 | 2:47:46 | 3:43:42 | 7:51:36 | 9:19:14 |
| 18:30 | 4:37 | 11:30 | 34:29 | 57:29 | 1:54:57 | 2:52:26 | 3:49:54 | 8:04:42 | 9:34:46 |
| 19:00 | 4:45 | 11:48 | 35:25 | 59:02 | 1:58:04 | 2:57:05 | 3:56:07 | 8:17:48 | 9:50:18 |
| 19:30 | 4:53 | 12:07 | 36:21 | 1:00:35 | 2:01:10 | 3:01:45 | 4:02:20 | 8:30:54 | 10:05:50 |
| 20:00 | 5:00 | 12:26 | 37:17 | 1:02:08 | 2:04:16 | 3:06:25 | 4:08:33 | 8:44:00 | 10:21:22 |

*"All glory comes from daring to begin."*

*Ancient proverb*

## **MON**DAY            DATE:_____   TIME OF DAY:_____   WEATHER:_____

COURSE/NOTES
_____
_____
_____
_____
_____

MORNING PULSE / WEIGHT                    MILES / TIME

---

## **TUES**DAY            DATE:_____   TIME OF DAY:_____   WEATHER:_____

COURSE/NOTES
_____
_____
_____
_____
_____

MORNING PULSE / WEIGHT                    MILES / TIME

---

## **WED**NESDAY            DATE:_____   TIME OF DAY:_____   WEATHER:_____

COURSE/NOTES
_____
_____
_____
_____
_____

MORNING PULSE / WEIGHT                    MILES / TIME

---

## **THU**RSDAY            DATE:_____   TIME OF DAY:_____   WEATHER:_____

COURSE/NOTES
_____
_____
_____
_____
_____

MORNING PULSE / WEIGHT                    MILES / TIME

DATE:_____ TIME OF DAY:_____ WEATHER:_____ **FRI**DAY

COURSE/NOTES
_____
_____
_____
_____
_____
_____

MORNING PULSE / WEIGHT　　　　　　　　　　　MILES / TIME

---

DATE:_____ TIME OF DAY:_____ WEATHER:_____ **SAT**URDAY

COURSE/NOTES
_____
_____
_____
_____
_____
_____

MORNING PULSE / WEIGHT　　　　　　　　　　　MILES / TIME

---

DATE:_____ TIME OF DAY:_____ WEATHER:_____ **SUN**DAY

COURSE/NOTES
_____
_____
_____
_____
_____
_____

MORNING PULSE / WEIGHT　　　　　　　　　　　MILES / TIME

---

## **ADDITIONAL** NOTES:

_____
_____
_____

| | |
|---|---|
| WEEKLY TOTAL | |
| PRIOR TOTAL | |
| CUMULATIVE TOTAL | |

## MONDAY

DATE:_____ TIME OF DAY:_____ WEATHER:_____

COURSE/NOTES

_____
_____
_____
_____
_____

MORNING PULSE / WEIGHT     MILES / TIME

## TUESDAY

DATE:_____ TIME OF DAY:_____ WEATHER:_____

COURSE/NOTES

_____
_____
_____
_____
_____

MORNING PULSE / WEIGHT     MILES / TIME

## WEDNESDAY

DATE:_____ TIME OF DAY:_____ WEATHER:_____

COURSE/NOTES

_____
_____
_____
_____
_____

MORNING PULSE / WEIGHT     MILES / TIME

## THURSDAY

DATE:_____ TIME OF DAY:_____ WEATHER:_____

COURSE/NOTES

_____
_____
_____
_____
_____

MORNING PULSE / WEIGHT     MILES / TIME

## **FRI**DAY

DATE:_____ TIME OF DAY:_____ WEATHER:_____

COURSE/NOTES
_____
_____
_____
_____
_____
_____

MORNING PULSE / WEIGHT  |  MILES / TIME

## **SAT**URDAY

DATE:_____ TIME OF DAY:_____ WEATHER:_____

COURSE/NOTES
_____
_____
_____
_____
_____
_____

MORNING PULSE / WEIGHT  |  MILES / TIME

## **SUN**DAY

DATE:_____ TIME OF DAY:_____ WEATHER:_____

COURSE/NOTES
_____
_____
_____
_____
_____
_____

MORNING PULSE / WEIGHT  |  MILES / TIME

## **ADDITIONAL** NOTES:

_____
_____

| | |
|---|---|
| WEEKLY TOTAL | |
| PRIOR TOTAL | |
| CUMULATIVE TOTAL | |

## **MON**DAY    DATE:_____ TIME OF DAY:_____ WEATHER:_____

COURSE/NOTES
_____
_____
_____
_____
_____

MORNING PULSE / WEIGHT           MILES / TIME


## **TUES**DAY    DATE:_____ TIME OF DAY:_____ WEATHER:_____

COURSE/NOTES
_____
_____
_____
_____
_____

MORNING PULSE / WEIGHT           MILES / TIME


## **WED**NESDAY    DATE:_____ TIME OF DAY:_____ WEATHER:_____

COURSE/NOTES
_____
_____
_____
_____
_____

MORNING PULSE / WEIGHT           MILES / TIME


## **THU**RSDAY    DATE:_____ TIME OF DAY:_____ WEATHER:_____

COURSE/NOTES
_____
_____
_____
_____
_____

MORNING PULSE / WEIGHT           MILES / TIME

## FRIDAY

DATE:_____ TIME OF DAY:_____ WEATHER:_____

COURSE/NOTES
_____
_____
_____
_____
_____

MORNING PULSE / WEIGHT [_____]  MILES / TIME [_____]

## SATURDAY

DATE:_____ TIME OF DAY:_____ WEATHER:_____

COURSE/NOTES
_____
_____
_____
_____
_____

MORNING PULSE / WEIGHT [_____]  MILES / TIME [_____]

## SUNDAY

DATE:_____ TIME OF DAY:_____ WEATHER:_____

COURSE/NOTES
_____
_____
_____
_____
_____

MORNING PULSE / WEIGHT [_____]  MILES / TIME [_____]

## ADDITIONAL NOTES:

_____
_____

| | |
|---|---|
| WEEKLY TOTAL | [_____] |
| PRIOR TOTAL | [_____] |
| CUMULATIVE TOTAL | [_____] |

## **MON**DAY

DATE:_____ TIME OF DAY:_____ WEATHER:_____

COURSE/NOTES

MORNING PULSE / WEIGHT

MILES / TIME

## **TUES**DAY

DATE:_____ TIME OF DAY:_____ WEATHER:_____

COURSE/NOTES

MORNING PULSE / WEIGHT

MILES / TIME

## **WED**NESDAY

DATE:_____ TIME OF DAY:_____ WEATHER:_____

COURSE/NOTES

MORNING PULSE / WEIGHT

MILES / TIME

## **THU**RSDAY

DATE:_____ TIME OF DAY:_____ WEATHER:_____

COURSE/NOTES

MORNING PULSE / WEIGHT

MILES / TIME

DATE:_____ TIME OF DAY:_____ WEATHER:_____ **FRI**DAY

COURSE/NOTES
_____
_____
_____
_____
_____

MORNING PULSE / WEIGHT        MILES / TIME

DATE:_____ TIME OF DAY:_____ WEATHER:_____ **SAT**URDAY

COURSE/NOTES
_____
_____
_____
_____
_____

MORNING PULSE / WEIGHT        MILES / TIME

DATE:_____ TIME OF DAY:_____ WEATHER:_____ **SUN**DAY

COURSE/NOTES
_____
_____
_____
_____
_____

MORNING PULSE / WEIGHT        MILES / TIME

## **ADDITIONAL** NOTES:

_____
_____

| | |
|---|---|
| WEEKLY TOTAL | |
| PRIOR TOTAL | |
| CUMULATIVE TOTAL | |

## **MON**DAY      DATE:_____ TIME OF DAY:_____ WEATHER:_____

COURSE/NOTES
_____
_____
_____
_____
_____

MORNING PULSE / WEIGHT [_____]          MILES / TIME [_____]


## **TUES**DAY      DATE:_____ TIME OF DAY:_____ WEATHER:_____

COURSE/NOTES
_____
_____
_____
_____
_____

MORNING PULSE / WEIGHT [_____]          MILES / TIME [_____]


## **WED**NESDAY      DATE:_____ TIME OF DAY:_____ WEATHER:_____

COURSE/NOTES
_____
_____
_____
_____
_____

MORNING PULSE / WEIGHT [_____]          MILES / TIME [_____]


## **THU**RSDAY      DATE:_____ TIME OF DAY:_____ WEATHER:_____

COURSE/NOTES
_____
_____
_____
_____
_____

MORNING PULSE / WEIGHT [_____]          MILES / TIME [_____]

DATE:_____ TIME OF DAY:_____ WEATHER:_____ **FRI**DAY

COURSE/NOTES
_____
_____
_____
_____
_____

MORNING PULSE / WEIGHT       MILES / TIME

DATE:_____ TIME OF DAY:_____ WEATHER:_____ **SAT**URDAY

COURSE/NOTES
_____
_____
_____
_____
_____

MORNING PULSE / WEIGHT       MILES / TIME

DATE:_____ TIME OF DAY:_____ WEATHER:_____ **SUN**DAY

COURSE/NOTES
_____
_____
_____
_____
_____

MORNING PULSE / WEIGHT       MILES / TIME

## **ADDITIONAL** NOTES:

_____
_____

| | |
|---|---|
| WEEKLY TOTAL | |
| PRIOR TOTAL | |
| CUMULATIVE TOTAL | |

## **MON**DAY       DATE:_____ TIME OF DAY:_____ WEATHER:_____

COURSE/NOTES
_____
_____
_____
_____
_____

MORNING PULSE / WEIGHT            MILES / TIME

## **TUES**DAY       DATE:_____ TIME OF DAY:_____ WEATHER:_____

COURSE/NOTES
_____
_____
_____
_____
_____

MORNING PULSE / WEIGHT            MILES / TIME

## **WED**NESDAY       DATE:_____ TIME OF DAY:_____ WEATHER:_____

COURSE/NOTES
_____
_____
_____
_____
_____

MORNING PULSE / WEIGHT            MILES / TIME

## **THU**RSDAY       DATE:_____ TIME OF DAY:_____ WEATHER:_____

COURSE/NOTES
_____
_____
_____
_____
_____

MORNING PULSE / WEIGHT            MILES / TIME

DATE:_____ TIME OF DAY:_____ WEATHER:_____ **FRI**DAY

COURSE/NOTES
_____
_____
_____
_____
_____
_____

MORNING PULSE / WEIGHT [_____]   MILES / TIME [_____]

---

DATE:_____ TIME OF DAY:_____ WEATHER:_____ **SAT**URDAY

COURSE/NOTES
_____
_____
_____
_____
_____
_____

MORNING PULSE / WEIGHT [_____]   MILES / TIME [_____]

---

DATE:_____ TIME OF DAY:_____ WEATHER:_____ **SUN**DAY

COURSE/NOTES
_____
_____
_____
_____
_____
_____

MORNING PULSE / WEIGHT [_____]   MILES / TIME [_____]

## **ADDITIONAL** NOTES:

_____
_____

| | | |
|---|---|---|
| _____ | WEEKLY TOTAL | [_____] |
| _____ | PRIOR TOTAL | [_____] |
| _____ | CUMULATIVE TOTAL | [_____] |

## **MON**DAY    DATE:_____  TIME OF DAY:_____  WEATHER:_____

COURSE/NOTES
_____
_____
_____
_____
_____

MORNING PULSE / WEIGHT    MILES / TIME

## **TUES**DAY   DATE:_____  TIME OF DAY:_____  WEATHER:_____

COURSE/NOTES
_____
_____
_____
_____
_____

MORNING PULSE / WEIGHT    MILES / TIME

## **WED**NESDAY   DATE:_____  TIME OF DAY:_____  WEATHER:_____

COURSE/NOTES
_____
_____
_____
_____
_____

MORNING PULSE / WEIGHT    MILES / TIME

## **THU**RSDAY   DATE:_____  TIME OF DAY:_____  WEATHER:_____

COURSE/NOTES
_____
_____
_____
_____
_____

MORNING PULSE / WEIGHT    MILES / TIME

DATE:_____ TIME OF DAY:_____ WEATHER:_____ **FRI**DAY

COURSE/NOTES
_____
_____
_____
_____
_____
_____

MORNING PULSE / WEIGHT [        ]          MILES / TIME [        ]

DATE:_____ TIME OF DAY:_____ WEATHER:_____ **SAT**URDAY

COURSE/NOTES
_____
_____
_____
_____
_____
_____

MORNING PULSE / WEIGHT [        ]          MILES / TIME [        ]

DATE:_____ TIME OF DAY:_____ WEATHER:_____ **SUN**DAY

COURSE/NOTES
_____
_____
_____
_____
_____
_____

MORNING PULSE / WEIGHT [        ]          MILES / TIME [        ]

## **ADDITIONAL** NOTES:

_____
_____
_____

| | |
|---|---|
| WEEKLY TOTAL | |
| PRIOR TOTAL | |
| CUMULATIVE TOTAL | |

*"She who has health has hope, and she who has hope has everything."*

Arabian proverb

"No one knows what he can
do until he tries."

*Latin proverb*

# **MON**DAY

DATE:_____ TIME OF DAY:_____ WEATHER:_____

COURSE/NOTES
_____
_____
_____
_____
_____

MORNING PULSE / WEIGHT   MILES / TIME

# **TUES**DAY

DATE:_____ TIME OF DAY:_____ WEATHER:_____

COURSE/NOTES
_____
_____
_____
_____
_____

MORNING PULSE / WEIGHT   MILES / TIME

# **WED**NESDAY

DATE:_____ TIME OF DAY:_____ WEATHER:_____

COURSE/NOTES
_____
_____
_____
_____
_____

MORNING PULSE / WEIGHT   MILES / TIME

# **THU**RSDAY

DATE:_____ TIME OF DAY:_____ WEATHER:_____

COURSE/NOTES
_____
_____
_____
_____
_____

MORNING PULSE / WEIGHT   MILES / TIME

DATE:_____ TIME OF DAY:_____ WEATHER:_____ **FRI**DAY

COURSE/NOTES
_____
_____
_____
_____
_____

MORNING PULSE / WEIGHT         MILES / TIME

---

DATE:_____ TIME OF DAY:_____ WEATHER:_____ **SAT**URDAY

COURSE/NOTES
_____
_____
_____
_____
_____

MORNING PULSE / WEIGHT         MILES / TIME

---

DATE:_____ TIME OF DAY:_____ WEATHER:_____ **SUN**DAY

COURSE/NOTES
_____
_____
_____
_____
_____

MORNING PULSE / WEIGHT         MILES / TIME

## **ADDITIONAL** NOTES:

_____
_____
_____

| | |
|---|---|
| WEEKLY TOTAL | |
| PRIOR TOTAL | |
| CUMULATIVE TOTAL | |

## **MON**DAY

DATE:_____ TIME OF DAY:_____ WEATHER:_____

COURSE/NOTES
_____
_____
_____
_____
_____
_____

MORNING PULSE / WEIGHT

MILES / TIME

## **TUES**DAY

DATE:_____ TIME OF DAY:_____ WEATHER:_____

COURSE/NOTES
_____
_____
_____
_____
_____
_____

MORNING PULSE / WEIGHT

MILES / TIME

## **WED**NESDAY

DATE:_____ TIME OF DAY:_____ WEATHER:_____

COURSE/NOTES
_____
_____
_____
_____
_____
_____

MORNING PULSE / WEIGHT

MILES / TIME

## **THU**RSDAY

DATE:_____ TIME OF DAY:_____ WEATHER:_____

COURSE/NOTES
_____
_____
_____
_____
_____
_____

MORNING PULSE / WEIGHT

MILES / TIME

DATE:_____ TIME OF DAY:_____ WEATHER:_____ **FRI**DAY

COURSE/NOTES
_____
_____
_____
_____
_____
_____

MORNING PULSE / WEIGHT          MILES / TIME


DATE:_____ TIME OF DAY:_____ WEATHER:_____ **SAT**URDAY

COURSE/NOTES
_____
_____
_____
_____
_____
_____

MORNING PULSE / WEIGHT          MILES / TIME


DATE:_____ TIME OF DAY:_____ WEATHER:_____ **SUN**DAY

COURSE/NOTES
_____
_____
_____
_____
_____
_____

MORNING PULSE / WEIGHT          MILES / TIME


## **ADDITIONAL** NOTES:

_____
_____
_____

| | |
|---|---|
| WEEKLY TOTAL | |
| PRIOR TOTAL | |
| CUMULATIVE TOTAL | |

## MONDAY

DATE:_____ TIME OF DAY:_____ WEATHER:_____

COURSE/NOTES
_____
_____
_____
_____
_____
_____

MORNING PULSE / WEIGHT  □       MILES / TIME  □

## TUESDAY

DATE:_____ TIME OF DAY:_____ WEATHER:_____

COURSE/NOTES
_____
_____
_____
_____
_____
_____

MORNING PULSE / WEIGHT  □       MILES / TIME  □

## WEDNESDAY

DATE:_____ TIME OF DAY:_____ WEATHER:_____

COURSE/NOTES
_____
_____
_____
_____
_____
_____

MORNING PULSE / WEIGHT  □       MILES / TIME  □

## THURSDAY

DATE:_____ TIME OF DAY:_____ WEATHER:_____

COURSE/NOTES
_____
_____
_____
_____
_____
_____

MORNING PULSE / WEIGHT  □       MILES / TIME  □

DATE:_____ TIME OF DAY:_____ WEATHER:_____ **FRI**DAY

COURSE/NOTES
_____
_____
_____
_____
_____
_____

MORNING PULSE / WEIGHT          MILES / TIME

---

DATE:_____ TIME OF DAY:_____ WEATHER:_____ **SAT**URDAY

COURSE/NOTES
_____
_____
_____
_____
_____
_____

MORNING PULSE / WEIGHT          MILES / TIME

---

DATE:_____ TIME OF DAY:_____ WEATHER:_____ **SUN**DAY

COURSE/NOTES
_____
_____
_____
_____
_____
_____

MORNING PULSE / WEIGHT          MILES / TIME

## **ADDITIONAL** NOTES:

_____
_____
_____

| | |
|---|---|
| WEEKLY TOTAL | |
| PRIOR TOTAL | |
| CUMULATIVE TOTAL | |

## **MON**DAY  DATE:_____ TIME OF DAY:_____ WEATHER:_____

COURSE/NOTES
_____
_____
_____
_____
_____

MORNING PULSE / WEIGHT           MILES / TIME

## **TUES**DAY  DATE:_____ TIME OF DAY:_____ WEATHER:_____

COURSE/NOTES
_____
_____
_____
_____
_____

MORNING PULSE / WEIGHT           MILES / TIME

## **WED**NESDAY  DATE:_____ TIME OF DAY:_____ WEATHER:_____

COURSE/NOTES
_____
_____
_____
_____
_____

MORNING PULSE / WEIGHT           MILES / TIME

## **THU**RSDAY  DATE:_____ TIME OF DAY:_____ WEATHER:_____

COURSE/NOTES
_____
_____
_____
_____
_____

MORNING PULSE / WEIGHT           MILES / TIME

DATE:_____ TIME OF DAY:_____ WEATHER:_____ **FRI**DAY

COURSE/NOTES

MORNING PULSE / WEIGHT

MILES / TIME

DATE:_____ TIME OF DAY:_____ WEATHER:_____ **SAT**URDAY

COURSE/NOTES

MORNING PULSE / WEIGHT

MILES / TIME

DATE:_____ TIME OF DAY:_____ WEATHER:_____ **SUN**DAY

COURSE/NOTES

MORNING PULSE / WEIGHT

MILES / TIME

**ADDITIONAL** NOTES:

WEEKLY TOTAL

PRIOR TOTAL

CUMULATIVE TOTAL

## **MON**DAY

DATE:_____ TIME OF DAY:_____ WEATHER:_____

COURSE/NOTES
_____
_____
_____
_____
_____

MORNING PULSE / WEIGHT [        ]    MILES / TIME [        ]


## **TUES**DAY

DATE:_____ TIME OF DAY:_____ WEATHER:_____

COURSE/NOTES
_____
_____
_____
_____
_____

MORNING PULSE / WEIGHT [        ]    MILES / TIME [        ]


## **WED**NESDAY

DATE:_____ TIME OF DAY:_____ WEATHER:_____

COURSE/NOTES
_____
_____
_____
_____
_____

MORNING PULSE / WEIGHT [        ]    MILES / TIME [        ]


## **THU**RSDAY

DATE:_____ TIME OF DAY:_____ WEATHER:_____

COURSE/NOTES
_____
_____
_____
_____
_____

MORNING PULSE / WEIGHT [        ]    MILES / TIME [        ]

DATE:_____ TIME OF DAY:_____ WEATHER:_____ **FRI**DAY

COURSE/NOTES
_____
_____
_____
_____
_____
_____

MORNING PULSE / WEIGHT          MILES / TIME

---

DATE:_____ TIME OF DAY:_____ WEATHER:_____ **SAT**URDAY

COURSE/NOTES
_____
_____
_____
_____
_____
_____

MORNING PULSE / WEIGHT          MILES / TIME

---

DATE:_____ TIME OF DAY:_____ WEATHER:_____ **SUN**DAY

COURSE/NOTES
_____
_____
_____
_____
_____
_____

MORNING PULSE / WEIGHT          MILES / TIME

---

## **ADDITIONAL** NOTES:

_____
_____
_____

| | |
|---|---|
| WEEKLY TOTAL | |
| PRIOR TOTAL | |
| CUMULATIVE TOTAL | |

## **MON**DAY      DATE:_____ TIME OF DAY:_____ WEATHER:_____

COURSE/NOTES
_____
_____
_____
_____
_____

MORNING PULSE / WEIGHT            MILES / TIME

## **TUES**DAY      DATE:_____ TIME OF DAY:_____ WEATHER:_____

COURSE/NOTES
_____
_____
_____
_____
_____

MORNING PULSE / WEIGHT            MILES / TIME

## **WED**NESDAY      DATE:_____ TIME OF DAY:_____ WEATHER:_____

COURSE/NOTES
_____
_____
_____
_____
_____

MORNING PULSE / WEIGHT            MILES / TIME

## **THU**RSDAY      DATE:_____ TIME OF DAY:_____ WEATHER:_____

COURSE/NOTES
_____
_____
_____
_____
_____

MORNING PULSE / WEIGHT            MILES / TIME

## FRIDAY

DATE:_____ TIME OF DAY:_____ WEATHER:_____

COURSE/NOTES
_____
_____
_____
_____
_____
_____

MORNING PULSE / WEIGHT  
MILES / TIME

## SATURDAY

DATE:_____ TIME OF DAY:_____ WEATHER:_____

COURSE/NOTES
_____
_____
_____
_____
_____
_____

MORNING PULSE / WEIGHT  
MILES / TIME

## SUNDAY

DATE:_____ TIME OF DAY:_____ WEATHER:_____

COURSE/NOTES
_____
_____
_____
_____
_____
_____

MORNING PULSE / WEIGHT  
MILES / TIME

## ADDITIONAL NOTES:

_____
_____
_____
_____
_____
_____

WEEKLY TOTAL  
PRIOR TOTAL  
CUMULATIVE TOTAL

## **MON**DAY

DATE:_____ TIME OF DAY:_____ WEATHER:_____

COURSE/NOTES

_____
_____
_____
_____
_____

MORNING PULSE / WEIGHT

MILES / TIME

## **TUES**DAY

DATE:_____ TIME OF DAY:_____ WEATHER:_____

COURSE/NOTES

_____
_____
_____
_____
_____

MORNING PULSE / WEIGHT

MILES / TIME

## **WED**NESDAY

DATE:_____ TIME OF DAY:_____ WEATHER:_____

COURSE/NOTES

_____
_____
_____
_____
_____

MORNING PULSE / WEIGHT

MILES / TIME

## **THU**RSDAY

DATE:_____ TIME OF DAY:_____ WEATHER:_____

COURSE/NOTES

_____
_____
_____
_____
_____

MORNING PULSE / WEIGHT

MILES / TIME

DATE:_____ TIME OF DAY:_____ WEATHER:_____ **FRI**DAY

COURSE/NOTES
_____
_____
_____
_____
_____
_____

MORNING PULSE / WEIGHT

MILES / TIME

---

DATE:_____ TIME OF DAY:_____ WEATHER:_____ **SAT**URDAY

COURSE/NOTES
_____
_____
_____
_____
_____
_____

MORNING PULSE / WEIGHT

MILES / TIME

---

DATE:_____ TIME OF DAY:_____ WEATHER:_____ **SUN**DAY

COURSE/NOTES
_____
_____
_____
_____
_____
_____

MORNING PULSE / WEIGHT

MILES / TIME

---

## **ADDITIONAL** NOTES:

_____
_____

| | |
|---|---|
| WEEKLY TOTAL | |
| PRIOR TOTAL | |
| CUMULATIVE TOTAL | |

"The greater the difficulty, the more glory in surmounting it."

*Epicurus*

"If I had known I was going to live this long, I would have taken better care of myself."

Unknown

## MONDAY

DATE:_____ TIME OF DAY:_____ WEATHER:_____

COURSE/NOTES

MORNING PULSE / WEIGHT

MILES / TIME

## TUESDAY

DATE:_____ TIME OF DAY:_____ WEATHER:_____

COURSE/NOTES

MORNING PULSE / WEIGHT

MILES / TIME

## WEDNESDAY

DATE: Nov 2  TIME OF DAY: 9:20  WEATHER: Cool/Cloudy

COURSE/NOTES
Walked around ponds to bridge + back.
with Sadie brisk walk.
20 min.
Calves ached.

MORNING PULSE / WEIGHT: 204

MILES / TIME: 20 min

## THURSDAY

DATE:_____ TIME OF DAY:_____ WEATHER:_____

COURSE/NOTES

MORNING PULSE / WEIGHT

MILES / TIME

DATE:_____ TIME OF DAY:_____ WEATHER:_____ **FRI**DAY

COURSE/NOTES
_____
_____
_____
_____
_____
_____

MORNING PULSE / WEIGHT            MILES / TIME

DATE:_____ TIME OF DAY:_____ WEATHER:_____ **SAT**URDAY

COURSE/NOTES
_____
_____
_____
_____
_____
_____

MORNING PULSE / WEIGHT            MILES / TIME

DATE:_____ TIME OF DAY:_____ WEATHER:_____ **SUN**DAY

COURSE/NOTES
_____
_____
_____
_____
_____
_____

MORNING PULSE / WEIGHT            MILES / TIME

**ADDITIONAL** NOTES:
_____
_____

| | |
|---|---|
| WEEKLY TOTAL | |
| PRIOR TOTAL | |
| CUMULATIVE TOTAL | |

## **MON**DAY

DATE:_____ TIME OF DAY:_____ WEATHER:_____

COURSE/NOTES
_____
_____
_____
_____
_____
_____

MORNING PULSE / WEIGHT

MILES / TIME

## **TUES**DAY

DATE:_____ TIME OF DAY:_____ WEATHER:_____

COURSE/NOTES
_____
_____
_____
_____
_____
_____

MORNING PULSE / WEIGHT

MILES / TIME

## **WED**NESDAY

DATE:_____ TIME OF DAY:_____ WEATHER:_____

COURSE/NOTES
_____
_____
_____
_____
_____
_____

MORNING PULSE / WEIGHT

MILES / TIME

## **THU**RSDAY

DATE:_____ TIME OF DAY:_____ WEATHER:_____

COURSE/NOTES
_____
_____
_____
_____
_____
_____

MORNING PULSE / WEIGHT

MILES / TIME

DATE:_____ TIME OF DAY:_____ WEATHER:_____ **FRI**DAY

COURSE/NOTES
_____
_____
_____
_____
_____
_____

MORNING PULSE / WEIGHT          MILES / TIME

---

DATE:_____ TIME OF DAY:_____ WEATHER:_____ **SAT**URDAY

COURSE/NOTES
_____
_____
_____
_____
_____
_____

MORNING PULSE / WEIGHT          MILES / TIME

---

DATE:_____ TIME OF DAY:_____ WEATHER:_____ **SUN**DAY

COURSE/NOTES
_____
_____
_____
_____
_____
_____

MORNING PULSE / WEIGHT          MILES / TIME

## **ADDITIONAL** NOTES:

_____
_____

| | |
|---|---|
| WEEKLY TOTAL | |
| PRIOR TOTAL | |
| CUMULATIVE TOTAL | |

# MONDAY

DATE:_____ TIME OF DAY:_____ WEATHER:_____

COURSE/NOTES
_____
_____
_____
_____
_____

MORNING PULSE / WEIGHT                    MILES / TIME

# TUESDAY

DATE:_____ TIME OF DAY:_____ WEATHER:_____

COURSE/NOTES
_____
_____
_____
_____
_____

MORNING PULSE / WEIGHT                    MILES / TIME

# WEDNESDAY

DATE:_____ TIME OF DAY:_____ WEATHER:_____

COURSE/NOTES
_____
_____
_____
_____
_____

MORNING PULSE / WEIGHT                    MILES / TIME

# THURSDAY

DATE:_____ TIME OF DAY:_____ WEATHER:_____

COURSE/NOTES
_____
_____
_____
_____
_____

MORNING PULSE / WEIGHT                    MILES / TIME

DATE:_____ TIME OF DAY:_____ WEATHER:_____ **FRI**DAY

COURSE/NOTES
_____
_____
_____
_____

MORNING PULSE / WEIGHT       MILES / TIME

DATE:_____ TIME OF DAY:_____ WEATHER:_____ **SAT**URDAY

COURSE/NOTES
_____
_____
_____
_____

MORNING PULSE / WEIGHT       MILES / TIME

DATE:_____ TIME OF DAY:_____ WEATHER:_____ **SUN**DAY

COURSE/NOTES
_____
_____
_____
_____

MORNING PULSE / WEIGHT       MILES / TIME

**ADDITIONAL** NOTES:

_____
_____

| | |
|---|---|
| WEEKLY TOTAL | |
| PRIOR TOTAL | |
| CUMULATIVE TOTAL | |

## MONDAY    DATE:_____ TIME OF DAY:_____ WEATHER:_____

COURSE/NOTES
_____
_____
_____
_____
_____

MORNING PULSE / WEIGHT [          ]    MILES / TIME [          ]

## TUESDAY    DATE:_____ TIME OF DAY:_____ WEATHER:_____

COURSE/NOTES
_____
_____
_____
_____
_____

MORNING PULSE / WEIGHT [          ]    MILES / TIME [          ]

## WEDNESDAY    DATE:_____ TIME OF DAY:_____ WEATHER:_____

COURSE/NOTES
_____
_____
_____
_____
_____

MORNING PULSE / WEIGHT [          ]    MILES / TIME [          ]

## THURSDAY    DATE:_____ TIME OF DAY:_____ WEATHER:_____

COURSE/NOTES
_____
_____
_____
_____
_____

MORNING PULSE / WEIGHT [          ]    MILES / TIME [          ]

DATE:_____ TIME OF DAY:_____ WEATHER:_____ **FRI**DAY

COURSE/NOTES
_____
_____
_____
_____
_____

MORNING PULSE / WEIGHT [          ]   MILES / TIME [          ]

DATE:_____ TIME OF DAY:_____ WEATHER:_____ **SAT**URDAY

COURSE/NOTES
_____
_____
_____
_____
_____

MORNING PULSE / WEIGHT [          ]   MILES / TIME [          ]

DATE:_____ TIME OF DAY:_____ WEATHER:_____ **SUN**DAY

COURSE/NOTES
_____
_____
_____
_____
_____

MORNING PULSE / WEIGHT [          ]   MILES / TIME [          ]

## **ADDITIONAL** NOTES:

_____
_____

| | |
|---|---|
| WEEKLY TOTAL | |
| PRIOR TOTAL | |
| CUMULATIVE TOTAL | |

## **MON**DAY  DATE:_____ TIME OF DAY:_____ WEATHER:_____

COURSE/NOTES
_____
_____
_____
_____
_____

MORNING PULSE / WEIGHT        MILES / TIME

## **TUES**DAY  DATE:_____ TIME OF DAY:_____ WEATHER:_____

COURSE/NOTES
_____
_____
_____
_____
_____

MORNING PULSE / WEIGHT        MILES / TIME

## **WED**NESDAY  DATE:_____ TIME OF DAY:_____ WEATHER:_____

COURSE/NOTES
_____
_____
_____
_____
_____

MORNING PULSE / WEIGHT        MILES / TIME

## **THU**RSDAY  DATE:_____ TIME OF DAY:_____ WEATHER:_____

COURSE/NOTES
_____
_____
_____
_____
_____

MORNING PULSE / WEIGHT        MILES / TIME

## **FRI**DAY

DATE:_____ TIME OF DAY:_____ WEATHER:_____

COURSE/NOTES
_____
_____
_____
_____
_____

MORNING PULSE / WEIGHT [        ]    MILES / TIME [        ]

## **SAT**URDAY

DATE:_____ TIME OF DAY:_____ WEATHER:_____

COURSE/NOTES
_____
_____
_____
_____
_____

MORNING PULSE / WEIGHT [        ]    MILES / TIME [        ]

## **SUN**DAY

DATE:_____ TIME OF DAY:_____ WEATHER:_____

COURSE/NOTES
_____
_____
_____
_____
_____

MORNING PULSE / WEIGHT [        ]    MILES / TIME [        ]

## **ADDITIONAL** NOTES:

_____
_____

| | |
|---|---|
| WEEKLY TOTAL | |
| PRIOR TOTAL | |
| CUMULATIVE TOTAL | |

## MONDAY

DATE:_____ TIME OF DAY:_____ WEATHER:_____

COURSE/NOTES
_____
_____
_____
_____
_____

MORNING PULSE / WEIGHT

MILES / TIME

## TUESDAY

DATE:_____ TIME OF DAY:_____ WEATHER:_____

COURSE/NOTES
_____
_____
_____
_____
_____

MORNING PULSE / WEIGHT

MILES / TIME

## WEDNESDAY

DATE:_____ TIME OF DAY:_____ WEATHER:_____

COURSE/NOTES
_____
_____
_____
_____
_____

MORNING PULSE / WEIGHT

MILES / TIME

## THURSDAY

DATE:_____ TIME OF DAY:_____ WEATHER:_____

COURSE/NOTES
_____
_____
_____
_____
_____

MORNING PULSE / WEIGHT

MILES / TIME

DATE:_____ TIME OF DAY:_____ WEATHER:_____ **FRI**DAY

COURSE/NOTES
_____
_____
_____
_____
_____

MORNING PULSE / WEIGHT                MILES / TIME

---

DATE:_____ TIME OF DAY:_____ WEATHER:_____ **SAT**URDAY

COURSE/NOTES
_____
_____
_____
_____
_____

MORNING PULSE / WEIGHT                MILES / TIME

---

DATE:_____ TIME OF DAY:_____ WEATHER:_____ **SUN**DAY

COURSE/NOTES
_____
_____
_____
_____
_____

MORNING PULSE / WEIGHT                MILES / TIME

---

## **ADDITIONAL** NOTES:

_____
_____

| | |
|---|---|
| WEEKLY TOTAL | |
| PRIOR TOTAL | |
| CUMULATIVE TOTAL | |

## MONDAY

DATE:_____ TIME OF DAY:_____ WEATHER:_____

COURSE/NOTES
_____
_____
_____
_____
_____

MORNING PULSE / WEIGHT

MILES / TIME

## TUESDAY

DATE:_____ TIME OF DAY:_____ WEATHER:_____

COURSE/NOTES
_____
_____
_____
_____
_____

MORNING PULSE / WEIGHT

MILES / TIME

## WEDNESDAY

DATE:_____ TIME OF DAY:_____ WEATHER:_____

COURSE/NOTES
_____
_____
_____
_____
_____

MORNING PULSE / WEIGHT

MILES / TIME

## THURSDAY

DATE:_____ TIME OF DAY:_____ WEATHER:_____

COURSE/NOTES
_____
_____
_____
_____
_____

MORNING PULSE / WEIGHT

MILES / TIME

DATE:_____ TIME OF DAY:_____ WEATHER:_____ **FRI**DAY

COURSE/NOTES
_____
_____
_____
_____
_____

MORNING PULSE / WEIGHT          MILES / TIME

---

DATE:_____ TIME OF DAY:_____ WEATHER:_____ **SAT**URDAY

COURSE/NOTES
_____
_____
_____
_____
_____

MORNING PULSE / WEIGHT          MILES / TIME

---

DATE:_____ TIME OF DAY:_____ WEATHER:_____ **SUN**DAY

COURSE/NOTES
_____
_____
_____
_____
_____

MORNING PULSE / WEIGHT          MILES / TIME

## **ADDITIONAL** NOTES:

_____
_____
_____

| | |
|---|---|
| WEEKLY TOTAL | |
| PRIOR TOTAL | |
| CUMULATIVE TOTAL | |

"The great thing in this world is not so much where we are, but in what direction we are moving."

*Oliver Wendell Holmes*

"The only reason I would take up jogging is so that I could hear heavy breathing again."

*Erma Bombeck*

## **MON**DAY      DATE:_____   TIME OF DAY:_____   WEATHER:_____

COURSE/NOTES
_____
_____
_____
_____
_____

MORNING PULSE / WEIGHT          MILES / TIME


## **TUES**DAY      DATE:_____   TIME OF DAY:_____   WEATHER:_____

COURSE/NOTES
_____
_____
_____
_____
_____

MORNING PULSE / WEIGHT          MILES / TIME


## **WED**NESDAY      DATE:_____   TIME OF DAY:_____   WEATHER:_____

COURSE/NOTES
_____
_____
_____
_____
_____

MORNING PULSE / WEIGHT          MILES / TIME


## **THU**RSDAY      DATE:_____   TIME OF DAY:_____   WEATHER:_____

COURSE/NOTES
_____
_____
_____
_____
_____

MORNING PULSE / WEIGHT          MILES / TIME

DATE:_____ TIME OF DAY:_____ WEATHER:_____ **FRI**DAY

COURSE/NOTES
_____
_____
_____
_____
_____
_____

MORNING PULSE / WEIGHT  [          ]          MILES / TIME  [          ]

---

DATE:_____ TIME OF DAY:_____ WEATHER:_____ **SAT**URDAY

COURSE/NOTES
_____
_____
_____
_____
_____
_____

MORNING PULSE / WEIGHT  [          ]          MILES / TIME  [          ]

---

DATE:_____ TIME OF DAY:_____ WEATHER:_____ **SUN**DAY

COURSE/NOTES
_____
_____
_____
_____
_____
_____

MORNING PULSE / WEIGHT  [          ]          MILES / TIME  [          ]

---

## **ADDITIONAL** NOTES:

_____
_____
_____

| | |
|---|---|
| _____ | |
| _____ | WEEKLY TOTAL [          ] |
| _____ | PRIOR TOTAL [          ] |
| _____ | CUMULATIVE TOTAL [          ] |
| _____ | |

## **MON**DAY   DATE:_____ TIME OF DAY:_____ WEATHER:_____

COURSE/NOTES
_____
_____
_____
_____
_____

MORNING PULSE / WEIGHT    MILES / TIME

---

## **TUES**DAY   DATE:_____ TIME OF DAY:_____ WEATHER:_____

COURSE/NOTES
_____
_____
_____
_____
_____

MORNING PULSE / WEIGHT    MILES / TIME

---

## **WED**NESDAY   DATE:_____ TIME OF DAY:_____ WEATHER:_____

COURSE/NOTES
_____
_____
_____
_____
_____

MORNING PULSE / WEIGHT    MILES / TIME

---

## **THU**RSDAY   DATE:_____ TIME OF DAY:_____ WEATHER:_____

COURSE/NOTES
_____
_____
_____
_____
_____

MORNING PULSE / WEIGHT    MILES / TIME

DATE:_____ TIME OF DAY:_____ WEATHER:_____ **FRI**DAY

COURSE/NOTES
_____
_____
_____
_____
_____
_____

MORNING PULSE / WEIGHT       MILES / TIME

DATE:_____ TIME OF DAY:_____ WEATHER:_____ **SAT**URDAY

COURSE/NOTES
_____
_____
_____
_____
_____
_____

MORNING PULSE / WEIGHT       MILES / TIME

DATE:_____ TIME OF DAY:_____ WEATHER:_____ **SUN**DAY

COURSE/NOTES
_____
_____
_____
_____
_____
_____

MORNING PULSE / WEIGHT       MILES / TIME

**ADDITIONAL** NOTES:
_____
_____
_____

| | |
|---|---|
| WEEKLY TOTAL | |
| PRIOR TOTAL | |
| CUMULATIVE TOTAL | |

# **MON**DAY

DATE:_____ TIME OF DAY:_____ WEATHER:_____

COURSE/NOTES
_____
_____
_____
_____
_____

MORNING PULSE / WEIGHT   MILES / TIME

# **TUES**DAY

DATE:_____ TIME OF DAY:_____ WEATHER:_____

COURSE/NOTES
_____
_____
_____
_____
_____

MORNING PULSE / WEIGHT   MILES / TIME

# **WED**NESDAY

DATE:_____ TIME OF DAY:_____ WEATHER:_____

COURSE/NOTES
_____
_____
_____
_____
_____

MORNING PULSE / WEIGHT   MILES / TIME

# **THU**RSDAY

DATE:_____ TIME OF DAY:_____ WEATHER:_____

COURSE/NOTES
_____
_____
_____
_____
_____

MORNING PULSE / WEIGHT   MILES / TIME

DATE:_____ TIME OF DAY:_____ WEATHER:_____ **FRI**DAY

COURSE/NOTES
_____
_____
_____
_____
_____

MORNING PULSE / WEIGHT [_____]   MILES / TIME [_____]

---

DATE:_____ TIME OF DAY:_____ WEATHER:_____ **SAT**URDAY

COURSE/NOTES
_____
_____
_____
_____
_____

MORNING PULSE / WEIGHT [_____]   MILES / TIME [_____]

---

DATE:_____ TIME OF DAY:_____ WEATHER:_____ **SUN**DAY

COURSE/NOTES
_____
_____
_____
_____
_____

MORNING PULSE / WEIGHT [_____]   MILES / TIME [_____]

## **ADDITIONAL** NOTES:

_____
_____

| | |
|---|---|
| WEEKLY TOTAL | |
| PRIOR TOTAL | |
| CUMULATIVE TOTAL | |

## **MON**DAY      DATE:_____ TIME OF DAY:_____ WEATHER:_____

COURSE/NOTES
_____
_____
_____
_____
_____

MORNING PULSE / WEIGHT            MILES / TIME

## **TUES**DAY      DATE:_____ TIME OF DAY:_____ WEATHER:_____

COURSE/NOTES
_____
_____
_____
_____
_____

MORNING PULSE / WEIGHT            MILES / TIME

## **WED**NESDAY      DATE:_____ TIME OF DAY:_____ WEATHER:_____

COURSE/NOTES
_____
_____
_____
_____
_____

MORNING PULSE / WEIGHT            MILES / TIME

## **THU**RSDAY      DATE:_____ TIME OF DAY:_____ WEATHER:_____

COURSE/NOTES
_____
_____
_____
_____
_____

MORNING PULSE / WEIGHT            MILES / TIME

DATE:_____ TIME OF DAY:_____ WEATHER:_____  **FRI**DAY

COURSE/NOTES
_____
_____
_____
_____
_____
_____

MORNING PULSE / WEIGHT

MILES / TIME

---

DATE:_____ TIME OF DAY:_____ WEATHER:_____  **SAT**URDAY

COURSE/NOTES
_____
_____
_____
_____
_____
_____

MORNING PULSE / WEIGHT

MILES / TIME

---

DATE:_____ TIME OF DAY:_____ WEATHER:_____  **SUN**DAY

COURSE/NOTES
_____
_____
_____
_____
_____
_____

MORNING PULSE / WEIGHT

MILES / TIME

---

## **ADDITIONAL** NOTES:

_____
_____
_____

| | |
|---|---|
| WEEKLY TOTAL | |
| PRIOR TOTAL | |
| CUMULATIVE TOTAL | |

## MONDAY

DATE:_____ TIME OF DAY:_____ WEATHER:_____

COURSE/NOTES
_____
_____
_____
_____
_____

MORNING PULSE / WEIGHT                    MILES / TIME

---

## TUESDAY

DATE:_____ TIME OF DAY:_____ WEATHER:_____

COURSE/NOTES
_____
_____
_____
_____
_____

MORNING PULSE / WEIGHT                    MILES / TIME

---

## WEDNESDAY

DATE:_____ TIME OF DAY:_____ WEATHER:_____

COURSE/NOTES
_____
_____
_____
_____
_____

MORNING PULSE / WEIGHT                    MILES / TIME

---

## THURSDAY

DATE:_____ TIME OF DAY:_____ WEATHER:_____

COURSE/NOTES
_____
_____
_____
_____
_____

MORNING PULSE / WEIGHT                    MILES / TIME

DATE:_____ TIME OF DAY:_____ WEATHER:_____  **FRI**DAY

COURSE/NOTES
_____
_____
_____
_____
_____

MORNING PULSE / WEIGHT          MILES / TIME

---

DATE:_____ TIME OF DAY:_____ WEATHER:_____  **SAT**URDAY

COURSE/NOTES
_____
_____
_____
_____
_____

MORNING PULSE / WEIGHT          MILES / TIME

---

DATE:_____ TIME OF DAY:_____ WEATHER:_____  **SUN**DAY

COURSE/NOTES
_____
_____
_____
_____
_____

MORNING PULSE / WEIGHT          MILES / TIME

---

**ADDITIONAL** NOTES:

_____
_____
_____

WEEKLY TOTAL

PRIOR TOTAL

CUMULATIVE TOTAL

## MONDAY       DATE:_____ TIME OF DAY:_____ WEATHER:_____

COURSE/NOTES
_____
_____
_____
_____
_____
_____

MORNING PULSE / WEIGHT                    MILES / TIME


## TUESDAY       DATE:_____ TIME OF DAY:_____ WEATHER:_____

COURSE/NOTES
_____
_____
_____
_____
_____
_____

MORNING PULSE / WEIGHT                    MILES / TIME


## WEDNESDAY       DATE:_____ TIME OF DAY:_____ WEATHER:_____

COURSE/NOTES
_____
_____
_____
_____
_____
_____

MORNING PULSE / WEIGHT                    MILES / TIME


## THURSDAY       DATE:_____ TIME OF DAY:_____ WEATHER:_____

COURSE/NOTES
_____
_____
_____
_____
_____
_____

MORNING PULSE / WEIGHT                    MILES / TIME

DATE:_____ TIME OF DAY:_____ WEATHER:_____ **FRI**DAY

COURSE/NOTES
_____
_____
_____
_____
_____
_____

MORNING PULSE / WEIGHT          MILES / TIME

DATE:_____ TIME OF DAY:_____ WEATHER:_____ **SAT**URDAY

COURSE/NOTES
_____
_____
_____
_____
_____
_____

MORNING PULSE / WEIGHT          MILES / TIME

DATE:_____ TIME OF DAY:_____ WEATHER:_____ **SUN**DAY

COURSE/NOTES
_____
_____
_____
_____
_____
_____

MORNING PULSE / WEIGHT          MILES / TIME

## **ADDITIONAL** NOTES:

_____
_____

| | |
|---|---|
| WEEKLY TOTAL | |
| PRIOR TOTAL | |
| CUMULATIVE TOTAL | |

## **MON**DAY           DATE:_____   TIME OF DAY:_____   WEATHER:_____

COURSE/NOTES
_____
_____
_____
_____
_____

MORNING PULSE / WEIGHT [_____]          MILES / TIME [_____]


## **TUES**DAY           DATE:_____   TIME OF DAY:_____   WEATHER:_____

COURSE/NOTES
_____
_____
_____
_____
_____

MORNING PULSE / WEIGHT [_____]          MILES / TIME [_____]


## **WED**NESDAY         DATE:_____   TIME OF DAY:_____   WEATHER:_____

COURSE/NOTES
_____
_____
_____
_____
_____

MORNING PULSE / WEIGHT [_____]          MILES / TIME [_____]


## **THU**RSDAY          DATE:_____   TIME OF DAY:_____   WEATHER:_____

COURSE/NOTES
_____
_____
_____
_____
_____

MORNING PULSE / WEIGHT [_____]          MILES / TIME [_____]

DATE:_____ TIME OF DAY:_____ WEATHER:_____ **FRI**DAY

COURSE/NOTES
_____
_____
_____
_____
_____

MORNING PULSE / WEIGHT  [            ]     MILES / TIME  [            ]

---

DATE:_____ TIME OF DAY:_____ WEATHER:_____ **SAT**URDAY

COURSE/NOTES
_____
_____
_____
_____
_____

MORNING PULSE / WEIGHT  [            ]     MILES / TIME  [            ]

---

DATE:_____ TIME OF DAY:_____ WEATHER:_____ **SUN**DAY

COURSE/NOTES
_____
_____
_____
_____
_____

MORNING PULSE / WEIGHT  [            ]     MILES / TIME  [            ]

---

## **ADDITIONAL** NOTES:

_____
_____
_____

| | |
|---|---|
| WEEKLY TOTAL | |
| PRIOR TOTAL | |
| CUMULATIVE TOTAL | |

"Heaven never helps those who will not act."

*Sophocles*

*"Progress comes from the intelligent use of experience."*

*Tom Landry*

## **MON**DAY

DATE:_____ TIME OF DAY:_____ WEATHER:_____

COURSE/NOTES
_____
_____
_____
_____
_____

MORNING PULSE / WEIGHT          MILES / TIME


## **TUES**DAY

DATE:_____ TIME OF DAY:_____ WEATHER:_____

COURSE/NOTES
_____
_____
_____
_____
_____

MORNING PULSE / WEIGHT          MILES / TIME


## **WED**NESDAY

DATE:_____ TIME OF DAY:_____ WEATHER:_____

COURSE/NOTES
_____
_____
_____
_____
_____

MORNING PULSE / WEIGHT          MILES / TIME


## **THU**RSDAY

DATE:_____ TIME OF DAY:_____ WEATHER:_____

COURSE/NOTES
_____
_____
_____
_____
_____

MORNING PULSE / WEIGHT          MILES / TIME

DATE:_____ TIME OF DAY:_____ WEATHER:_____ **FRI**DAY

COURSE/NOTES
_____
_____
_____
_____
_____
_____

MORNING PULSE / WEIGHT  [        ]          MILES / TIME  [        ]

DATE:_____ TIME OF DAY:_____ WEATHER:_____ **SAT**URDAY

COURSE/NOTES
_____
_____
_____
_____
_____
_____

MORNING PULSE / WEIGHT  [        ]          MILES / TIME  [        ]

DATE:_____ TIME OF DAY:_____ WEATHER:_____ **SUN**DAY

COURSE/NOTES
_____
_____
_____
_____
_____
_____

MORNING PULSE / WEIGHT  [        ]          MILES / TIME  [        ]

## **ADDITIONAL** NOTES:

_____
_____

| | |
|---|---|
| WEEKLY TOTAL | |
| PRIOR TOTAL | |
| CUMULATIVE TOTAL | |

## **MON**DAY

DATE:_____ TIME OF DAY:_____ WEATHER:_____

COURSE/NOTES

_____
_____
_____
_____
_____

MORNING PULSE / WEIGHT     MILES / TIME

## **TUES**DAY

DATE:_____ TIME OF DAY:_____ WEATHER:_____

COURSE/NOTES

_____
_____
_____
_____
_____

MORNING PULSE / WEIGHT     MILES / TIME

## **WED**NESDAY

DATE:_____ TIME OF DAY:_____ WEATHER:_____

COURSE/NOTES

_____
_____
_____
_____
_____

MORNING PULSE / WEIGHT     MILES / TIME

## **THU**RSDAY

DATE:_____ TIME OF DAY:_____ WEATHER:_____

COURSE/NOTES

_____
_____
_____
_____
_____

MORNING PULSE / WEIGHT     MILES / TIME

## **FRI**DAY

DATE:_____ TIME OF DAY:_____ WEATHER:_____

COURSE/NOTES
_____
_____
_____
_____
_____

MORNING PULSE / WEIGHT [          ]     MILES / TIME [          ]

---

## **SAT**URDAY

DATE:_____ TIME OF DAY:_____ WEATHER:_____

COURSE/NOTES
_____
_____
_____
_____
_____

MORNING PULSE / WEIGHT [          ]     MILES / TIME [          ]

---

## **SUN**DAY

DATE:_____ TIME OF DAY:_____ WEATHER:_____

COURSE/NOTES
_____
_____
_____
_____
_____

MORNING PULSE / WEIGHT [          ]     MILES / TIME [          ]

## **ADDITIONAL** NOTES:

_____
_____

| | |
|---|---|
| WEEKLY TOTAL | |
| PRIOR TOTAL | |
| CUMULATIVE TOTAL | |

## **MON**DAY        DATE:_____    TIME OF DAY:_____    WEATHER:_____

COURSE/NOTES
_____
_____
_____
_____
_____

MORNING PULSE / WEIGHT [          ]        MILES / TIME [          ]


## **TUES**DAY        DATE:_____    TIME OF DAY:_____    WEATHER:_____

COURSE/NOTES
_____
_____
_____
_____
_____

MORNING PULSE / WEIGHT [          ]        MILES / TIME [          ]


## **WED**NESDAY        DATE:_____    TIME OF DAY:_____    WEATHER:_____

COURSE/NOTES
_____
_____
_____
_____
_____

MORNING PULSE / WEIGHT [          ]        MILES / TIME [          ]


## **THU**RSDAY        DATE:_____    TIME OF DAY:_____    WEATHER:_____

COURSE/NOTES
_____
_____
_____
_____
_____

MORNING PULSE / WEIGHT [          ]        MILES / TIME [          ]

DATE:_____ TIME OF DAY:_____ WEATHER:_____ **FRI**DAY

COURSE/NOTES
_____
_____
_____
_____
_____

MORNING PULSE / WEIGHT          MILES / TIME

DATE:_____ TIME OF DAY:_____ WEATHER:_____ **SAT**URDAY

COURSE/NOTES
_____
_____
_____
_____
_____

MORNING PULSE / WEIGHT          MILES / TIME

DATE:_____ TIME OF DAY:_____ WEATHER:_____ **SUN**DAY

COURSE/NOTES
_____
_____
_____
_____
_____

MORNING PULSE / WEIGHT          MILES / TIME

**ADDITIONAL** NOTES:
_____
_____

| | |
|---|---|
| WEEKLY TOTAL | |
| PRIOR TOTAL | |
| CUMULATIVE TOTAL | |

# **MON**DAY

DATE:_____ TIME OF DAY:_____ WEATHER:_____

COURSE/NOTES
_____
_____
_____
_____
_____

MORNING PULSE / WEIGHT

MILES / TIME

# **TUES**DAY

DATE:_____ TIME OF DAY:_____ WEATHER:_____

COURSE/NOTES
_____
_____
_____
_____
_____

MORNING PULSE / WEIGHT

MILES / TIME

# **WED**NESDAY

DATE:_____ TIME OF DAY:_____ WEATHER:_____

COURSE/NOTES
_____
_____
_____
_____
_____

MORNING PULSE / WEIGHT

MILES / TIME

# **THU**RSDAY

DATE:_____ TIME OF DAY:_____ WEATHER:_____

COURSE/NOTES
_____
_____
_____
_____
_____

MORNING PULSE / WEIGHT

MILES / TIME

DATE:_____ TIME OF DAY:_____ WEATHER:_____ **FRI**DAY

COURSE/NOTES
_____
_____
_____
_____
_____

MORNING PULSE / WEIGHT       MILES / TIME

DATE:_____ TIME OF DAY:_____ WEATHER:_____ **SAT**URDAY

COURSE/NOTES
_____
_____
_____
_____
_____

MORNING PULSE / WEIGHT       MILES / TIME

DATE:_____ TIME OF DAY:_____ WEATHER:_____ **SUN**DAY

COURSE/NOTES
_____
_____
_____
_____
_____

MORNING PULSE / WEIGHT       MILES / TIME

## **ADDITIONAL** NOTES:

_____
_____

| | |
|---|---|
| WEEKLY TOTAL | |
| PRIOR TOTAL | |
| CUMULATIVE TOTAL | |

## **MON**DAY

DATE:_____ TIME OF DAY:_____ WEATHER:_____

COURSE/NOTES
_____
_____
_____
_____
_____

MORNING PULSE / WEIGHT          MILES / TIME


## **TUES**DAY

DATE:_____ TIME OF DAY:_____ WEATHER:_____

COURSE/NOTES
_____
_____
_____
_____
_____

MORNING PULSE / WEIGHT          MILES / TIME


## **WED**NESDAY

DATE:_____ TIME OF DAY:_____ WEATHER:_____

COURSE/NOTES
_____
_____
_____
_____
_____

MORNING PULSE / WEIGHT          MILES / TIME


## **THU**RSDAY

DATE:_____ TIME OF DAY:_____ WEATHER:_____

COURSE/NOTES
_____
_____
_____
_____
_____

MORNING PULSE / WEIGHT          MILES / TIME

## **FRI**DAY

DATE:_____ TIME OF DAY:_____ WEATHER:_____

COURSE/NOTES
_____
_____
_____
_____
_____
_____

MORNING PULSE / WEIGHT

MILES / TIME

## **SAT**URDAY

DATE:_____ TIME OF DAY:_____ WEATHER:_____

COURSE/NOTES
_____
_____
_____
_____
_____
_____

MORNING PULSE / WEIGHT

MILES / TIME

## **SUN**DAY

DATE:_____ TIME OF DAY:_____ WEATHER:_____

COURSE/NOTES
_____
_____
_____
_____
_____
_____

MORNING PULSE / WEIGHT

MILES / TIME

## **ADDITIONAL** NOTES:

_____
_____
_____

| | |
|---|---|
| WEEKLY TOTAL | |
| PRIOR TOTAL | |
| CUMULATIVE TOTAL | |

# **MON**DAY

DATE:_____ TIME OF DAY:_____ WEATHER:_____

COURSE/NOTES
_____
_____
_____
_____
_____
_____

MORNING PULSE / WEIGHT            MILES / TIME

# **TUES**DAY

DATE:_____ TIME OF DAY:_____ WEATHER:_____

COURSE/NOTES
_____
_____
_____
_____
_____
_____

MORNING PULSE / WEIGHT            MILES / TIME

# **WED**NESDAY

DATE:_____ TIME OF DAY:_____ WEATHER:_____

COURSE/NOTES
_____
_____
_____
_____
_____
_____

MORNING PULSE / WEIGHT            MILES / TIME

# **THU**RSDAY

DATE:_____ TIME OF DAY:_____ WEATHER:_____

COURSE/NOTES
_____
_____
_____
_____
_____
_____

MORNING PULSE / WEIGHT            MILES / TIME

DATE:_____ TIME OF DAY:_____ WEATHER:_____ **FRI**DAY

COURSE/NOTES
_____
_____
_____
_____
_____
_____

MORNING PULSE / WEIGHT

MILES / TIME

---

DATE:_____ TIME OF DAY:_____ WEATHER:_____ **SAT**URDAY

COURSE/NOTES
_____
_____
_____
_____
_____
_____

MORNING PULSE / WEIGHT

MILES / TIME

---

DATE:_____ TIME OF DAY:_____ WEATHER:_____ **SUN**DAY

COURSE/NOTES
_____
_____
_____
_____
_____
_____

MORNING PULSE / WEIGHT

MILES / TIME

---

## **ADDITIONAL** NOTES:

_____
_____

| | |
|---|---|
| WEEKLY TOTAL | |
| PRIOR TOTAL | |
| CUMULATIVE TOTAL | |

## **MON**DAY   DATE:_____ TIME OF DAY:_____ WEATHER:_____

COURSE/NOTES
_____
_____
_____
_____
_____

MORNING PULSE / WEIGHT          MILES / TIME

## **TUES**DAY   DATE:_____ TIME OF DAY:_____ WEATHER:_____

COURSE/NOTES
_____
_____
_____
_____
_____

MORNING PULSE / WEIGHT          MILES / TIME

## **WED**NESDAY   DATE:_____ TIME OF DAY:_____ WEATHER:_____

COURSE/NOTES
_____
_____
_____
_____
_____

MORNING PULSE / WEIGHT          MILES / TIME

## **THU**RSDAY   DATE:_____ TIME OF DAY:_____ WEATHER:_____

COURSE/NOTES
_____
_____
_____
_____
_____

MORNING PULSE / WEIGHT          MILES / TIME

DATE:_____ TIME OF DAY:_____ WEATHER:_____ **FRI**DAY

COURSE/NOTES
_____
_____
_____
_____
_____
_____

MORNING PULSE / WEIGHT                              MILES / TIME

---

DATE:_____ TIME OF DAY:_____ WEATHER:_____ **SAT**URDAY

COURSE/NOTES
_____
_____
_____
_____
_____
_____

MORNING PULSE / WEIGHT                              MILES / TIME

---

DATE:_____ TIME OF DAY:_____ WEATHER:_____ **SUN**DAY

COURSE/NOTES
_____
_____
_____
_____
_____
_____

MORNING PULSE / WEIGHT                              MILES / TIME

## **ADDITIONAL** NOTES:

_____
_____
_____

| | |
|---|---|
| WEEKLY TOTAL | |
| PRIOR TOTAL | |
| CUMULATIVE TOTAL | |

*"Never give in. Never. Never. Never. Never."*

Winston Churchill

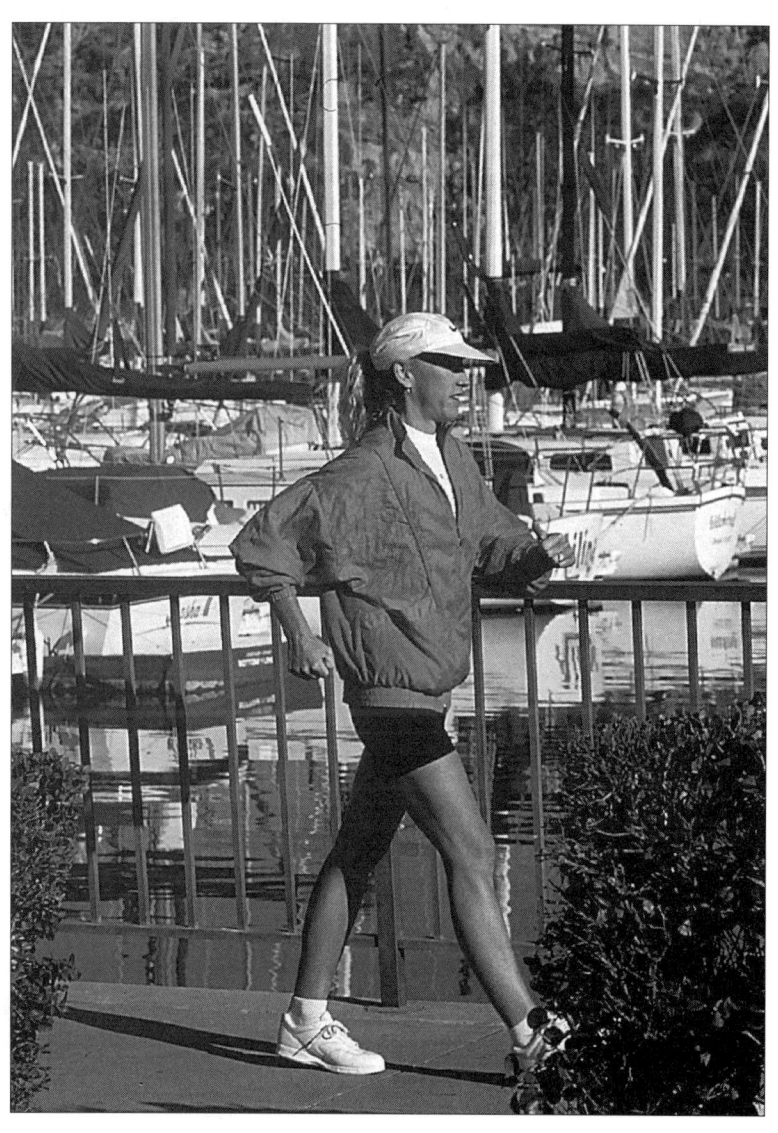

"Never eat more than you can lift."

Miss Piggy

## **MON**DAY    DATE:_____  TIME OF DAY:_____  WEATHER:_____

COURSE/NOTES
_____
_____
_____
_____
_____
_____

MORNING PULSE / WEIGHT            MILES / TIME

## **TUES**DAY    DATE:_____  TIME OF DAY:_____  WEATHER:_____

COURSE/NOTES
_____
_____
_____
_____
_____
_____

MORNING PULSE / WEIGHT            MILES / TIME

## **WED**NESDAY    DATE:_____  TIME OF DAY:_____  WEATHER:_____

COURSE/NOTES
_____
_____
_____
_____
_____
_____

MORNING PULSE / WEIGHT            MILES / TIME

## **THU**RSDAY    DATE:_____  TIME OF DAY:_____  WEATHER:_____

COURSE/NOTES
_____
_____
_____
_____
_____
_____

MORNING PULSE / WEIGHT            MILES / TIME

DATE:_____ TIME OF DAY:_____ WEATHER:_____ **FRI**DAY

COURSE/NOTES
_____
_____
_____
_____
_____
_____

MORNING PULSE / WEIGHT        MILES / TIME

---

DATE:_____ TIME OF DAY:_____ WEATHER:_____ **SAT**URDAY

COURSE/NOTES
_____
_____
_____
_____
_____
_____

MORNING PULSE / WEIGHT        MILES / TIME

---

DATE:_____ TIME OF DAY:_____ WEATHER:_____ **SUN**DAY

COURSE/NOTES
_____
_____
_____
_____
_____
_____

MORNING PULSE / WEIGHT        MILES / TIME

## **ADDITIONAL** NOTES:

_____
_____
_____

| | |
|---|---|
| WEEKLY TOTAL | |
| PRIOR TOTAL | |
| CUMULATIVE TOTAL | |

## MONDAY

DATE:_____ TIME OF DAY:_____ WEATHER:_____

COURSE/NOTES
_____
_____
_____
_____
_____

MORNING PULSE / WEIGHT

MILES / TIME

## TUESDAY

DATE:_____ TIME OF DAY:_____ WEATHER:_____

COURSE/NOTES
_____
_____
_____
_____
_____

MORNING PULSE / WEIGHT

MILES / TIME

## WEDNESDAY

DATE:_____ TIME OF DAY:_____ WEATHER:_____

COURSE/NOTES
_____
_____
_____
_____
_____

MORNING PULSE / WEIGHT

MILES / TIME

## THURSDAY

DATE:_____ TIME OF DAY:_____ WEATHER:_____

COURSE/NOTES
_____
_____
_____
_____
_____

MORNING PULSE / WEIGHT

MILES / TIME

DATE:_____ TIME OF DAY:_____ WEATHER:_____ **FRI**DAY

COURSE/NOTES
_____
_____
_____
_____
_____
_____

MORNING PULSE / WEIGHT  [          ]     MILES / TIME  [          ]


DATE:_____ TIME OF DAY:_____ WEATHER:_____ **SAT**URDAY

COURSE/NOTES
_____
_____
_____
_____
_____
_____

MORNING PULSE / WEIGHT  [          ]     MILES / TIME  [          ]


DATE:_____ TIME OF DAY:_____ WEATHER:_____ **SUN**DAY

COURSE/NOTES
_____
_____
_____
_____
_____
_____

MORNING PULSE / WEIGHT  [          ]     MILES / TIME  [          ]


## **ADDITIONAL** NOTES:
_____
_____

| | |
|---|---|
| _____ | |
| _____ | WEEKLY TOTAL [          ] |
| _____ | PRIOR TOTAL [          ] |
| _____ | CUMULATIVE TOTAL [          ] |
| _____ | |

## **MON**DAY          DATE:_____ TIME OF DAY:_____ WEATHER:_____
COURSE/NOTES
_____
_____
_____
_____
_____

MORNING PULSE / WEIGHT          MILES / TIME

## **TUES**DAY          DATE:_____ TIME OF DAY:_____ WEATHER:_____
COURSE/NOTES
_____
_____
_____
_____
_____

MORNING PULSE / WEIGHT          MILES / TIME

## **WED**NESDAY          DATE:_____ TIME OF DAY:_____ WEATHER:_____
COURSE/NOTES
_____
_____
_____
_____
_____

MORNING PULSE / WEIGHT          MILES / TIME

## **THU**RSDAY          DATE:_____ TIME OF DAY:_____ WEATHER:_____
COURSE/NOTES
_____
_____
_____
_____
_____

MORNING PULSE / WEIGHT          MILES / TIME

DATE:_____ TIME OF DAY:_____ WEATHER:_____ **FRI**DAY

COURSE/NOTES
_____
_____
_____
_____
_____

MORNING PULSE / WEIGHT  [          ]        MILES / TIME  [          ]

---

DATE:_____ TIME OF DAY:_____ WEATHER:_____ **SAT**URDAY

COURSE/NOTES
_____
_____
_____
_____
_____

MORNING PULSE / WEIGHT  [          ]        MILES / TIME  [          ]

---

DATE:_____ TIME OF DAY:_____ WEATHER:_____ **SUN**DAY

COURSE/NOTES
_____
_____
_____
_____
_____

MORNING PULSE / WEIGHT  [          ]        MILES / TIME  [          ]

---

**ADDITIONAL** NOTES:
_____
_____

| | |
|---|---|
| WEEKLY TOTAL | |
| PRIOR TOTAL | |
| CUMULATIVE TOTAL | |

## **MON**DAY       DATE:_____  TIME OF DAY:_____  WEATHER:_____

COURSE/NOTES
_____
_____
_____
_____
_____

MORNING PULSE / WEIGHT            MILES / TIME

## **TUES**DAY       DATE:_____  TIME OF DAY:_____  WEATHER:_____

COURSE/NOTES
_____
_____
_____
_____
_____

MORNING PULSE / WEIGHT            MILES / TIME

## **WED**NESDAY       DATE:_____  TIME OF DAY:_____  WEATHER:_____

COURSE/NOTES
_____
_____
_____
_____
_____

MORNING PULSE / WEIGHT            MILES / TIME

## **THU**RSDAY       DATE:_____  TIME OF DAY:_____  WEATHER:_____

COURSE/NOTES
_____
_____
_____
_____
_____

MORNING PULSE / WEIGHT            MILES / TIME

DATE:_____ TIME OF DAY:_____ WEATHER:_____ **FRI**DAY

COURSE/NOTES
_____
_____
_____
_____
_____
_____

MORNING PULSE / WEIGHT        MILES / TIME


DATE:_____ TIME OF DAY:_____ WEATHER:_____ **SAT**URDAY

COURSE/NOTES
_____
_____
_____
_____
_____
_____

MORNING PULSE / WEIGHT        MILES / TIME


DATE:_____ TIME OF DAY:_____ WEATHER:_____ **SUN**DAY

COURSE/NOTES
_____
_____
_____
_____
_____
_____

MORNING PULSE / WEIGHT        MILES / TIME


## **ADDITIONAL** NOTES:

_____
_____

| | |
|---|---|
| WEEKLY TOTAL | |
| PRIOR TOTAL | |
| CUMULATIVE TOTAL | |

## **MON**DAY

DATE:_____ TIME OF DAY:_____ WEATHER:_____

COURSE/NOTES
_____
_____
_____
_____
_____

MORNING PULSE / WEIGHT      MILES / TIME

---

## **TUES**DAY

DATE:_____ TIME OF DAY:_____ WEATHER:_____

COURSE/NOTES
_____
_____
_____
_____
_____

MORNING PULSE / WEIGHT      MILES / TIME

---

## **WED**NESDAY

DATE:_____ TIME OF DAY:_____ WEATHER:_____

COURSE/NOTES
_____
_____
_____
_____
_____

MORNING PULSE / WEIGHT      MILES / TIME

---

## **THU**RSDAY

DATE:_____ TIME OF DAY:_____ WEATHER:_____

COURSE/NOTES
_____
_____
_____
_____
_____

MORNING PULSE / WEIGHT      MILES / TIME

DATE:_____ TIME OF DAY:_____ WEATHER:_____ **FRI**DAY

COURSE/NOTES
_____
_____
_____
_____
_____

MORNING PULSE / WEIGHT  MILES / TIME

---

DATE:_____ TIME OF DAY:_____ WEATHER:_____ **SAT**URDAY

COURSE/NOTES
_____
_____
_____
_____
_____

MORNING PULSE / WEIGHT  MILES / TIME

---

DATE:_____ TIME OF DAY:_____ WEATHER:_____ **SUN**DAY

COURSE/NOTES
_____
_____
_____
_____
_____

MORNING PULSE / WEIGHT  MILES / TIME

## **ADDITIONAL** NOTES:

_____
_____

| | |
|---|---|
| WEEKLY TOTAL | |
| PRIOR TOTAL | |
| CUMULATIVE TOTAL | |

## **MON**DAY

DATE:_____ TIME OF DAY:_____ WEATHER:_____

COURSE/NOTES
_____
_____
_____
_____
_____

MORNING PULSE / WEIGHT            MILES / TIME

## **TUES**DAY

DATE:_____ TIME OF DAY:_____ WEATHER:_____

COURSE/NOTES
_____
_____
_____
_____
_____

MORNING PULSE / WEIGHT            MILES / TIME

## **WED**NESDAY

DATE:_____ TIME OF DAY:_____ WEATHER:_____

COURSE/NOTES
_____
_____
_____
_____
_____

MORNING PULSE / WEIGHT            MILES / TIME

## **THU**RSDAY

DATE:_____ TIME OF DAY:_____ WEATHER:_____

COURSE/NOTES
_____
_____
_____
_____
_____

MORNING PULSE / WEIGHT            MILES / TIME

DATE:_____ TIME OF DAY:_____ WEATHER:_____ **FRI**DAY

COURSE/NOTES
_____
_____
_____
_____
_____
_____

MORNING PULSE / WEIGHT          MILES / TIME

---

DATE:_____ TIME OF DAY:_____ WEATHER:_____ **SAT**URDAY

COURSE/NOTES
_____
_____
_____
_____
_____
_____

MORNING PULSE / WEIGHT          MILES / TIME

---

DATE:_____ TIME OF DAY:_____ WEATHER:_____ **SUN**DAY

COURSE/NOTES
_____
_____
_____
_____
_____
_____

MORNING PULSE / WEIGHT          MILES / TIME

## **ADDITIONAL** NOTES:

_____
_____

| | |
|---|---|
| WEEKLY TOTAL | |
| PRIOR TOTAL | |
| CUMULATIVE TOTAL | |

## **MON**DAY

DATE:_____ TIME OF DAY:_____ WEATHER:_____

COURSE/NOTES
_____
_____
_____
_____
_____

MORNING PULSE / WEIGHT          MILES / TIME

## **TUES**DAY

DATE:_____ TIME OF DAY:_____ WEATHER:_____

COURSE/NOTES
_____
_____
_____
_____
_____

MORNING PULSE / WEIGHT          MILES / TIME

## **WED**NESDAY

DATE:_____ TIME OF DAY:_____ WEATHER:_____

COURSE/NOTES
_____
_____
_____
_____
_____

MORNING PULSE / WEIGHT          MILES / TIME

## **THU**RSDAY

DATE:_____ TIME OF DAY:_____ WEATHER:_____

COURSE/NOTES
_____
_____
_____
_____
_____

MORNING PULSE / WEIGHT          MILES / TIME

DATE:_____ TIME OF DAY:_____ WEATHER:_____ **FRI**DAY

COURSE/NOTES
_____
_____
_____
_____
_____

MORNING PULSE / WEIGHT          MILES / TIME

---

DATE:_____ TIME OF DAY:_____ WEATHER:_____ **SAT**URDAY

COURSE/NOTES
_____
_____
_____
_____
_____

MORNING PULSE / WEIGHT          MILES / TIME

---

DATE:_____ TIME OF DAY:_____ WEATHER:_____ **SUN**DAY

COURSE/NOTES
_____
_____
_____
_____
_____

MORNING PULSE / WEIGHT          MILES / TIME

---

## **ADDITIONAL** NOTES:

_____
_____
_____

| | |
|---|---|
| WEEKLY TOTAL | |
| PRIOR TOTAL | |
| CUMULATIVE TOTAL | |

*"A big shot is just a little shot who kept on shooting."*

Zig Ziglar

*"The secret of staying young is to live honestly, eat slowly, and lie about your age."*

Lucille Ball

## **MON**DAY  DATE:_____ TIME OF DAY:_____ WEATHER:_____

COURSE/NOTES
_____
_____
_____
_____
_____

MORNING PULSE / WEIGHT        MILES / TIME

## **TUES**DAY  DATE:_____ TIME OF DAY:_____ WEATHER:_____

COURSE/NOTES
_____
_____
_____
_____
_____

MORNING PULSE / WEIGHT        MILES / TIME

## **WED**NESDAY  DATE:_____ TIME OF DAY:_____ WEATHER:_____

COURSE/NOTES
_____
_____
_____
_____
_____

MORNING PULSE / WEIGHT        MILES / TIME

## **THU**RSDAY  DATE:_____ TIME OF DAY:_____ WEATHER:_____

COURSE/NOTES
_____
_____
_____
_____
_____

MORNING PULSE / WEIGHT        MILES / TIME

DATE:_____ TIME OF DAY:_____ WEATHER:_____ **FRI**DAY

COURSE/NOTES
_____
_____
_____
_____
_____
_____

MORNING PULSE / WEIGHT  [        ]     MILES / TIME  [        ]

DATE:_____ TIME OF DAY:_____ WEATHER:_____ **SAT**URDAY

COURSE/NOTES
_____
_____
_____
_____
_____
_____

MORNING PULSE / WEIGHT  [        ]     MILES / TIME  [        ]

DATE:_____ TIME OF DAY:_____ WEATHER:_____ **SUN**DAY

COURSE/NOTES
_____
_____
_____
_____
_____
_____

MORNING PULSE / WEIGHT  [        ]     MILES / TIME  [        ]

## **ADDITIONAL** NOTES:

_____
_____

| | |
|---|---|
| WEEKLY TOTAL | |
| PRIOR TOTAL | |
| CUMULATIVE TOTAL | |

## **MON**DAY

DATE:_____ TIME OF DAY:_____ WEATHER:_____

COURSE/NOTES
_____
_____
_____
_____
_____

MORNING PULSE / WEIGHT          MILES / TIME

## **TUES**DAY

DATE:_____ TIME OF DAY:_____ WEATHER:_____

COURSE/NOTES
_____
_____
_____
_____
_____

MORNING PULSE / WEIGHT          MILES / TIME

## **WED**NESDAY

DATE:_____ TIME OF DAY:_____ WEATHER:_____

COURSE/NOTES
_____
_____
_____
_____
_____

MORNING PULSE / WEIGHT          MILES / TIME

## **THU**RSDAY

DATE:_____ TIME OF DAY:_____ WEATHER:_____

COURSE/NOTES
_____
_____
_____
_____
_____

MORNING PULSE / WEIGHT          MILES / TIME

DATE:_____ TIME OF DAY:_____ WEATHER:_____ **FRI**DAY

COURSE/NOTES
_____
_____
_____
_____
_____

MORNING PULSE / WEIGHT               MILES / TIME

---

DATE:_____ TIME OF DAY:_____ WEATHER:_____ **SAT**URDAY

COURSE/NOTES
_____
_____
_____
_____
_____

MORNING PULSE / WEIGHT               MILES / TIME

---

DATE:_____ TIME OF DAY:_____ WEATHER:_____ **SUN**DAY

COURSE/NOTES
_____
_____
_____
_____
_____

MORNING PULSE / WEIGHT               MILES / TIME

## **ADDITIONAL** NOTES:

_____
_____

| | |
|---|---|
| WEEKLY TOTAL | |
| PRIOR TOTAL | |
| CUMULATIVE TOTAL | |

## **MON**DAY

DATE:_____ TIME OF DAY:_____ WEATHER:_____

COURSE/NOTES
_____
_____
_____
_____
_____

MORNING PULSE / WEIGHT

MILES / TIME

## **TUES**DAY

DATE:_____ TIME OF DAY:_____ WEATHER:_____

COURSE/NOTES
_____
_____
_____
_____
_____

MORNING PULSE / WEIGHT

MILES / TIME

## **WED**NESDAY

DATE:_____ TIME OF DAY:_____ WEATHER:_____

COURSE/NOTES
_____
_____
_____
_____
_____

MORNING PULSE / WEIGHT

MILES / TIME

## **THU**RSDAY

DATE:_____ TIME OF DAY:_____ WEATHER:_____

COURSE/NOTES
_____
_____
_____
_____
_____

MORNING PULSE / WEIGHT

MILES / TIME

DATE:_____ TIME OF DAY:_____ WEATHER:_____ **FRI**DAY

COURSE/NOTES
_____
_____
_____
_____
_____
_____

MORNING PULSE / WEIGHT [         ]       MILES / TIME [         ]


DATE:_____ TIME OF DAY:_____ WEATHER:_____ **SAT**URDAY

COURSE/NOTES
_____
_____
_____
_____
_____
_____

MORNING PULSE / WEIGHT [         ]       MILES / TIME [         ]


DATE:_____ TIME OF DAY:_____ WEATHER:_____ **SUN**DAY

COURSE/NOTES
_____
_____
_____
_____
_____
_____

MORNING PULSE / WEIGHT [         ]       MILES / TIME [         ]


## **ADDITIONAL** NOTES:

_____
_____

| | | |
|---|---|---|
| _____ | WEEKLY TOTAL | |
| _____ | PRIOR TOTAL | |
| _____ | CUMULATIVE TOTAL | |
| _____ | | |

## **MON**DAY    DATE:_____ TIME OF DAY:_____ WEATHER:_____

COURSE/NOTES

_____
_____
_____
_____
_____

MORNING PULSE / WEIGHT          MILES / TIME

---

## **TUES**DAY    DATE:_____ TIME OF DAY:_____ WEATHER:_____

COURSE/NOTES

_____
_____
_____
_____
_____

MORNING PULSE / WEIGHT          MILES / TIME

---

## **WED**NESDAY    DATE:_____ TIME OF DAY:_____ WEATHER:_____

COURSE/NOTES

_____
_____
_____
_____
_____

MORNING PULSE / WEIGHT          MILES / TIME

---

## **THU**RSDAY    DATE:_____ TIME OF DAY:_____ WEATHER:_____

COURSE/NOTES

_____
_____
_____
_____
_____

MORNING PULSE / WEIGHT          MILES / TIME

DATE:_____ TIME OF DAY:_____ WEATHER:_____ **FRI**DAY

COURSE/NOTES
_____
_____
_____
_____
_____

MORNING PULSE / WEIGHT    MILES / TIME

---

DATE:_____ TIME OF DAY:_____ WEATHER:_____ **SAT**URDAY

COURSE/NOTES
_____
_____
_____
_____
_____

MORNING PULSE / WEIGHT    MILES / TIME

---

DATE:_____ TIME OF DAY:_____ WEATHER:_____ **SUN**DAY

COURSE/NOTES
_____
_____
_____
_____
_____

MORNING PULSE / WEIGHT    MILES / TIME

## **ADDITIONAL** NOTES:

_____

| | |
|---|---|
| WEEKLY TOTAL | |
| PRIOR TOTAL | |
| CUMULATIVE TOTAL | |

## MONDAY

DATE:_____ TIME OF DAY:_____ WEATHER:_____

COURSE/NOTES
_____
_____
_____
_____
_____

MORNING PULSE / WEIGHT                    MILES / TIME


## TUESDAY

DATE:_____ TIME OF DAY:_____ WEATHER:_____

COURSE/NOTES
_____
_____
_____
_____
_____

MORNING PULSE / WEIGHT                    MILES / TIME


## WEDNESDAY

DATE:_____ TIME OF DAY:_____ WEATHER:_____

COURSE/NOTES
_____
_____
_____
_____
_____

MORNING PULSE / WEIGHT                    MILES / TIME


## THURSDAY

DATE:_____ TIME OF DAY:_____ WEATHER:_____

COURSE/NOTES
_____
_____
_____
_____
_____

MORNING PULSE / WEIGHT                    MILES / TIME

DATE:_____ TIME OF DAY:_____ WEATHER:_____ **FRI**DAY

COURSE/NOTES
_____
_____
_____
_____
_____
_____

MORNING PULSE / WEIGHT    MILES / TIME

---

DATE:_____ TIME OF DAY:_____ WEATHER:_____ **SAT**URDAY

COURSE/NOTES
_____
_____
_____
_____
_____
_____

MORNING PULSE / WEIGHT    MILES / TIME

---

DATE:_____ TIME OF DAY:_____ WEATHER:_____ **SUN**DAY

COURSE/NOTES
_____
_____
_____
_____
_____
_____

MORNING PULSE / WEIGHT    MILES / TIME

---

## **ADDITIONAL** NOTES:

_____
_____

| | |
|---|---|
| WEEKLY TOTAL | |
| PRIOR TOTAL | |
| CUMULATIVE TOTAL | |

## **MON**DAY  DATE:_____ TIME OF DAY:_____ WEATHER:_____

COURSE/NOTES
_____
_____
_____
_____
_____

MORNING PULSE / WEIGHT [        ]   MILES / TIME [        ]


## **TUES**DAY  DATE:_____ TIME OF DAY:_____ WEATHER:_____

COURSE/NOTES
_____
_____
_____
_____
_____

MORNING PULSE / WEIGHT [        ]   MILES / TIME [        ]


## **WED**NESDAY  DATE:_____ TIME OF DAY:_____ WEATHER:_____

COURSE/NOTES
_____
_____
_____
_____
_____

MORNING PULSE / WEIGHT [        ]   MILES / TIME [        ]


## **THU**RSDAY  DATE:_____ TIME OF DAY:_____ WEATHER:_____

COURSE/NOTES
_____
_____
_____
_____
_____

MORNING PULSE / WEIGHT [        ]   MILES / TIME [        ]

DATE:_____ TIME OF DAY:_____ WEATHER:_____  **FRI**DAY

COURSE/NOTES
_____
_____
_____
_____
_____
_____

MORNING PULSE / WEIGHT [          ]   MILES / TIME [          ]

---

DATE:_____ TIME OF DAY:_____ WEATHER:_____  **SAT**URDAY

COURSE/NOTES
_____
_____
_____
_____
_____
_____

MORNING PULSE / WEIGHT [          ]   MILES / TIME [          ]

---

DATE:_____ TIME OF DAY:_____ WEATHER:_____  **SUN**DAY

COURSE/NOTES
_____
_____
_____
_____
_____
_____

MORNING PULSE / WEIGHT [          ]   MILES / TIME [          ]

## **ADDITIONAL** NOTES:

_____
_____

| | |
|---|---|
| WEEKLY TOTAL | |
| PRIOR TOTAL | |
| CUMULATIVE TOTAL | |

## **MON**DAY

DATE:_____ TIME OF DAY:_____ WEATHER:_____

COURSE/NOTES
_____
_____
_____
_____
_____

MORNING PULSE / WEIGHT       MILES / TIME

## **TUES**DAY

DATE:_____ TIME OF DAY:_____ WEATHER:_____

COURSE/NOTES
_____
_____
_____
_____
_____

MORNING PULSE / WEIGHT       MILES / TIME

## **WED**NESDAY

DATE:_____ TIME OF DAY:_____ WEATHER:_____

COURSE/NOTES
_____
_____
_____
_____
_____

MORNING PULSE / WEIGHT       MILES / TIME

## **THU**RSDAY

DATE:_____ TIME OF DAY:_____ WEATHER:_____

COURSE/NOTES
_____
_____
_____
_____
_____

MORNING PULSE / WEIGHT       MILES / TIME

DATE:_____ TIME OF DAY:_____ WEATHER:_____ **FRI**DAY

COURSE/NOTES
_____
_____
_____
_____
_____
_____

MORNING PULSE / WEIGHT          MILES / TIME

---

DATE:_____ TIME OF DAY:_____ WEATHER:_____ **SAT**URDAY

COURSE/NOTES
_____
_____
_____
_____
_____
_____

MORNING PULSE / WEIGHT          MILES / TIME

---

DATE:_____ TIME OF DAY:_____ WEATHER:_____ **SUN**DAY

COURSE/NOTES
_____
_____
_____
_____
_____
_____

MORNING PULSE / WEIGHT          MILES / TIME

---

## **ADDITIONAL** NOTES:

_____
_____

| | |
|---|---|
| WEEKLY TOTAL | |
| PRIOR TOTAL | |
| CUMULATIVE TOTAL | |

"Do not follow where the path may lead. Go instead where there is no path, and leave a trail."

*Unknown*

"I've been on a diet for two weeks, and all I've lost is two weeks."

Totie Fields

## MONDAY  DATE:_____ TIME OF DAY:_____ WEATHER:_____

COURSE/NOTES
_____
_____
_____
_____
_____

MORNING PULSE / WEIGHT          MILES / TIME

## TUESDAY  DATE:_____ TIME OF DAY:_____ WEATHER:_____

COURSE/NOTES
_____
_____
_____
_____
_____

MORNING PULSE / WEIGHT          MILES / TIME

## WEDNESDAY  DATE:_____ TIME OF DAY:_____ WEATHER:_____

COURSE/NOTES
_____
_____
_____
_____
_____

MORNING PULSE / WEIGHT          MILES / TIME

## THURSDAY  DATE:_____ TIME OF DAY:_____ WEATHER:_____

COURSE/NOTES
_____
_____
_____
_____
_____

MORNING PULSE / WEIGHT          MILES / TIME

DATE:_____ TIME OF DAY:_____ WEATHER:_____ **FRI**DAY

COURSE/NOTES
_____
_____
_____
_____
_____
_____

MORNING PULSE / WEIGHT  MILES / TIME

---

DATE:_____ TIME OF DAY:_____ WEATHER:_____ **SAT**URDAY

COURSE/NOTES
_____
_____
_____
_____
_____
_____

MORNING PULSE / WEIGHT  MILES / TIME

---

DATE:_____ TIME OF DAY:_____ WEATHER:_____ **SUN**DAY

COURSE/NOTES
_____
_____
_____
_____
_____
_____

MORNING PULSE / WEIGHT  MILES / TIME

## **ADDITIONAL** NOTES:

_____
_____
_____

WEEKLY TOTAL

PRIOR TOTAL

CUMULATIVE TOTAL

## **MON**DAY

DATE:_____ TIME OF DAY:_____ WEATHER:_____

COURSE/NOTES
_____
_____
_____
_____
_____

MORNING PULSE / WEIGHT          MILES / TIME


## **TUES**DAY

DATE:_____ TIME OF DAY:_____ WEATHER:_____

COURSE/NOTES
_____
_____
_____
_____
_____

MORNING PULSE / WEIGHT          MILES / TIME


## **WED**NESDAY

DATE:_____ TIME OF DAY:_____ WEATHER:_____

COURSE/NOTES
_____
_____
_____
_____
_____

MORNING PULSE / WEIGHT          MILES / TIME


## **THU**RSDAY

DATE:_____ TIME OF DAY:_____ WEATHER:_____

COURSE/NOTES
_____
_____
_____
_____
_____

MORNING PULSE / WEIGHT          MILES / TIME

DATE:_____ TIME OF DAY:_____ WEATHER:_____ **FRI**DAY

COURSE/NOTES
_____
_____
_____
_____
_____

MORNING PULSE / WEIGHT    MILES / TIME

---

DATE:_____ TIME OF DAY:_____ WEATHER:_____ **SAT**URDAY

COURSE/NOTES
_____
_____
_____
_____
_____

MORNING PULSE / WEIGHT    MILES / TIME

---

DATE:_____ TIME OF DAY:_____ WEATHER:_____ **SUN**DAY

COURSE/NOTES
_____
_____
_____
_____
_____

MORNING PULSE / WEIGHT    MILES / TIME

---

## **ADDITIONAL** NOTES:

_____
_____

| | |
|---|---|
| _____ | WEEKLY TOTAL |
| _____ | PRIOR TOTAL |
| _____ | CUMULATIVE TOTAL |

## **MON**DAY

DATE:_____ TIME OF DAY:_____ WEATHER:_____

COURSE/NOTES

_____
_____
_____
_____
_____

MORNING PULSE / WEIGHT                    MILES / TIME

## **TUES**DAY

DATE:_____ TIME OF DAY:_____ WEATHER:_____

COURSE/NOTES

_____
_____
_____
_____
_____

MORNING PULSE / WEIGHT                    MILES / TIME

## **WED**NESDAY

DATE:_____ TIME OF DAY:_____ WEATHER:_____

COURSE/NOTES

_____
_____
_____
_____
_____

MORNING PULSE / WEIGHT                    MILES / TIME

## **THU**RSDAY

DATE:_____ TIME OF DAY:_____ WEATHER:_____

COURSE/NOTES

_____
_____
_____
_____
_____

MORNING PULSE / WEIGHT                    MILES / TIME

DATE:_____ TIME OF DAY:_____ WEATHER:_____ **FRI**DAY

COURSE/NOTES
_____
_____
_____
_____
_____
_____

MORNING PULSE / WEIGHT          MILES / TIME

---

DATE:_____ TIME OF DAY:_____ WEATHER:_____ **SAT**URDAY

COURSE/NOTES
_____
_____
_____
_____
_____
_____

MORNING PULSE / WEIGHT          MILES / TIME

---

DATE:_____ TIME OF DAY:_____ WEATHER:_____ **SUN**DAY

COURSE/NOTES
_____
_____
_____
_____
_____
_____

MORNING PULSE / WEIGHT          MILES / TIME

---

**ADDITIONAL** NOTES:

_____
_____

| | |
|---|---|
| WEEKLY TOTAL | |
| PRIOR TOTAL | |
| CUMULATIVE TOTAL | |

## **MON**DAY

DATE:_____ TIME OF DAY:_____ WEATHER:_____

COURSE/NOTES

_____
_____
_____
_____
_____

MORNING PULSE / WEIGHT

MILES / TIME

---

## **TUES**DAY

DATE:_____ TIME OF DAY:_____ WEATHER:_____

COURSE/NOTES

_____
_____
_____
_____
_____

MORNING PULSE / WEIGHT

MILES / TIME

---

## **WED**NESDAY

DATE:_____ TIME OF DAY:_____ WEATHER:_____

COURSE/NOTES

_____
_____
_____
_____
_____

MORNING PULSE / WEIGHT

MILES / TIME

---

## **THU**RSDAY

DATE:_____ TIME OF DAY:_____ WEATHER:_____

COURSE/NOTES

_____
_____
_____
_____
_____

MORNING PULSE / WEIGHT

MILES / TIME

DATE:_____ TIME OF DAY:_____ WEATHER:_____ **FRI**DAY

COURSE/NOTES
_____
_____
_____
_____
_____

MORNING PULSE / WEIGHT        MILES / TIME

---

DATE:_____ TIME OF DAY:_____ WEATHER:_____ **SAT**URDAY

COURSE/NOTES
_____
_____
_____
_____
_____

MORNING PULSE / WEIGHT        MILES / TIME

---

DATE:_____ TIME OF DAY:_____ WEATHER:_____ **SUN**DAY

COURSE/NOTES
_____
_____
_____
_____
_____

MORNING PULSE / WEIGHT        MILES / TIME

---

## **ADDITIONAL** NOTES:

_____
_____
_____

| | |
|---|---|
| WEEKLY TOTAL | |
| PRIOR TOTAL | |
| CUMULATIVE TOTAL | |

## **MON**DAY

DATE:_____ TIME OF DAY:_____ WEATHER:_____

COURSE/NOTES
_____
_____
_____
_____
_____

MORNING PULSE / WEIGHT  |  MILES / TIME

## **TUES**DAY

DATE:_____ TIME OF DAY:_____ WEATHER:_____

COURSE/NOTES
_____
_____
_____
_____
_____

MORNING PULSE / WEIGHT  |  MILES / TIME

## **WED**NESDAY

DATE:_____ TIME OF DAY:_____ WEATHER:_____

COURSE/NOTES
_____
_____
_____
_____
_____

MORNING PULSE / WEIGHT  |  MILES / TIME

## **THU**RSDAY

DATE:_____ TIME OF DAY:_____ WEATHER:_____

COURSE/NOTES
_____
_____
_____
_____
_____

MORNING PULSE / WEIGHT  |  MILES / TIME

## FRIDAY

DATE:_____ TIME OF DAY:_____ WEATHER:_____

COURSE/NOTES
_____
_____
_____
_____
_____

MORNING PULSE / WEIGHT  [         ]          MILES / TIME  [         ]

## SATURDAY

DATE:_____ TIME OF DAY:_____ WEATHER:_____

COURSE/NOTES
_____
_____
_____
_____
_____

MORNING PULSE / WEIGHT  [         ]          MILES / TIME  [         ]

## SUNDAY

DATE:_____ TIME OF DAY:_____ WEATHER:_____

COURSE/NOTES
_____
_____
_____
_____
_____

MORNING PULSE / WEIGHT  [         ]          MILES / TIME  [         ]

## ADDITIONAL NOTES:

_____
_____
_____

| | |
|---|---|
| WEEKLY TOTAL | |
| PRIOR TOTAL | |
| CUMULATIVE TOTAL | |

## **MON**DAY        DATE:_____ TIME OF DAY:_____ WEATHER:_____

COURSE/NOTES
_____
_____
_____
_____
_____

MORNING PULSE / WEIGHT          MILES / TIME

---

## **TUES**DAY       DATE:_____ TIME OF DAY:_____ WEATHER:_____

COURSE/NOTES
_____
_____
_____
_____
_____

MORNING PULSE / WEIGHT          MILES / TIME

---

## **WED**NESDAY     DATE:_____ TIME OF DAY:_____ WEATHER:_____

COURSE/NOTES
_____
_____
_____
_____
_____

MORNING PULSE / WEIGHT          MILES / TIME

---

## **THU**RSDAY      DATE:_____ TIME OF DAY:_____ WEATHER:_____

COURSE/NOTES
_____
_____
_____
_____
_____

MORNING PULSE / WEIGHT          MILES / TIME

DATE:_____ TIME OF DAY:_____ WEATHER:_____ **FRI**DAY

COURSE/NOTES
_____
_____
_____
_____
_____

MORNING PULSE / WEIGHT         MILES / TIME

DATE:_____ TIME OF DAY:_____ WEATHER:_____ **SAT**URDAY

COURSE/NOTES
_____
_____
_____
_____
_____

MORNING PULSE / WEIGHT         MILES / TIME

DATE:_____ TIME OF DAY:_____ WEATHER:_____ **SUN**DAY

COURSE/NOTES
_____
_____
_____
_____
_____

MORNING PULSE / WEIGHT         MILES / TIME

**ADDITIONAL** NOTES:

| | |
|---|---|
| WEEKLY TOTAL | |
| PRIOR TOTAL | |
| CUMULATIVE TOTAL | |

## MONDAY

DATE:_____ TIME OF DAY:_____ WEATHER:_____

COURSE/NOTES
_____
_____
_____
_____
_____
_____

MORNING PULSE / WEIGHT          MILES / TIME

## TUESDAY

DATE:_____ TIME OF DAY:_____ WEATHER:_____

COURSE/NOTES
_____
_____
_____
_____
_____
_____

MORNING PULSE / WEIGHT          MILES / TIME

## WEDNESDAY

DATE:_____ TIME OF DAY:_____ WEATHER:_____

COURSE/NOTES
_____
_____
_____
_____
_____
_____

MORNING PULSE / WEIGHT          MILES / TIME

## THURSDAY

DATE:_____ TIME OF DAY:_____ WEATHER:_____

COURSE/NOTES
_____
_____
_____
_____
_____
_____

MORNING PULSE / WEIGHT          MILES / TIME

DATE:_____ TIME OF DAY:_____ WEATHER:_____ **FRI**DAY

COURSE/NOTES
_____
_____
_____
_____
_____

MORNING PULSE / WEIGHT [          ]   MILES / TIME [          ]

DATE:_____ TIME OF DAY:_____ WEATHER:_____ **SAT**URDAY

COURSE/NOTES
_____
_____
_____
_____
_____

MORNING PULSE / WEIGHT [          ]   MILES / TIME [          ]

DATE:_____ TIME OF DAY:_____ WEATHER:_____ **SUN**DAY

COURSE/NOTES
_____
_____
_____
_____
_____

MORNING PULSE / WEIGHT [          ]   MILES / TIME [          ]

## **ADDITIONAL** NOTES:

_____
_____

| | |
|---|---|
| _____ | WEEKLY TOTAL [          ] |
| _____ | PRIOR TOTAL [          ] |
| _____ | CUMULATIVE TOTAL [          ] |

"You are today where your thoughts have brought you. You will be tomorrow where your thoughts take you."

James Allen